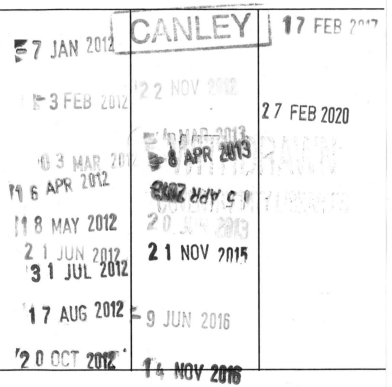

CASEY WATSON

The Boy No One Loved

This book is a work of non-fiction based on the author's experiences.
In order to protect privacy, names, identifying characteristics,
dialogue and details have been changed or reconstructed.

HarperElement
An Imprint of HarperCollins*Publishers*
77–85 Fulham Palace Road,
Hammersmith, London W6 8JB

www.harpercollins.co.uk

and *HarperElement* are trademarks of
HarperCollins*Publishers* Ltd

First published by HarperElement 2011

1 3 5 7 9 10 8 6 4 2

© Casey Watson 2011

Casey Watson asserts the moral right to
be identified as the author of this work

A catalogue record of this book
is available from the British Library

ISBN 978-0-00-743656-9

Printed and bound in Great Britain by
Clays Ltd, St Ives plc

MIX

FSC™ is a ... international organisation established to promote
the respon... ...ement of the world's forests. Products carrying the
FSC label a... ...e independently certified to assure consumers that they ...ne
from ... ...the social, economic and
...ological needs of present and future generations,

Find ...out more about HarperCollins and the environment at
www.harpercollins.co.uk/green

To my wonderful and supportive family

Acknowledgements

I would like to thank all of the team at HarperCollins, the lovely Andrew Lownie, and my friend and mentor, Lynne.

Prologue

His little brothers, the boy saw, were both covered in shit. They'd removed their full nappies and smeared each other in it, while their mother's dog – a spiteful brown terrier – was busy licking what remained from the bars of their shared cot.

He shooed the dog away and, gagging now, lifted both boys out, and then went to fetch a quilt from his mother's bedroom. Where had she gone this time? Why was she never there?

He took the boys downstairs, used the quilt to wrap them up warmly on the couch, and tuned the TV to a channel that was showing cartoons. 'We're hungry,' the older one kept repeating plaintively. 'We're hungry, Justin. Please Justin. Find us some food.'

There was nothing. There never was. Though he looked for some anyway. In all the cupboards. In the drawers. In the big dirty fridge. He felt tears spring in his eyes. And he also felt anger. He looked at his little brothers, at their hopeful, expectant faces. What was he supposed to feed them with? What was he supposed to do?

Then, suddenly, in that instant of despair, there came clarity. He didn't have to think. He knew *exactly* what to do. As if on autopilot now, he took his brothers out into the front garden, sat them down on the grass – still wrapped in the grubby quilt – and told them to stay where they were.

He then returned to the house and looked around the living room for the lighter. Picking it up, he calmly flicked it at the couch. He continued to do this till the couch began burning and then he went and set fire to the curtains.

The dog came downstairs then, its face all smeared with the contents of the brothers' nappies. The boy ran to the kitchen, to the cupboard under the sink, where there was a container of fluid which he knew was for the lighter. Grabbing this, he returned to the living room again, and squirted the fuel all over the animal's filthy face.

Taking one last look around, he walked out of the front door, closing it carefully behind him. He then joined his brothers under the quilt, on the grass, and calmly watched while both home and dog perished.

His mother was located, by the police, three hours later. She'd apparently spent the day at a friend's house. The little boy was just five and a half years old.

Chapter 1

Funny the little details that tend to stick in your mind, isn't it? The day Justin, the first foster child to ever be placed with us, was due to arrive – a bright but chilly day on the last Saturday before Christmas – all I kept going back to were the same old two things. One of them was just how desperate the social worker seemed to be that we should agree to have him, and the other was the fact that I had black hair.

And it wasn't just me either. My daughter Riley, now 21 and so supportive of the whole project from day one, had the same head of black hair that I did. We'd both of us inherited our raven locks from my mother and one thing I knew – and I really knew so little about Justin – was that he had a very powerful aversion to women with black hair.

I straightened his England football-team-themed duvet cover for the umpteenth time that morning, and tried to put the negative thoughts right out of my mind. I was trained to do this job, I told myself. So was my husband,

Mike. Plus I already had several years of experience looking after difficult children. And this was the new career I'd chosen for myself, wasn't it?

But along with the anxiety, I also felt proud. I looked around me and found myself smiling with satisfaction at what I saw. I certainly couldn't have thought harder about the way to do his new bedroom. Because one of the few things we did know was that Justin liked football, we quickly settled on that as a theme. So we'd done out the spare room in black and white and splashed out on some special wallpaper that made one of the walls look like it was a crowd at a stadium. We'd laid a green carpet, for a pitch, added a football-themed frieze, and I'd trawled charity shops endlessly for the books, games and jigsaws that I knew my own kids had enjoyed at his age. We also knew he liked movies, especially Disney films, apparently, so we'd bought him a starter pack of those too. I had agonised over every detail, every decision, every tiny item, because it meant so much to me to do everything I could to help him feel at home. The one thing I didn't know was what team he supported, so, till I did know, I'd pinched my son Kieron's old duvet cover for him. I reasoned that England was a pretty safe bet for any football-mad eleven-year-old boy.

I checked the time on the big blue clock Mike had fixed on the wall. Almost eleven. They would be here any minute, I realised. And, as if by magic, I heard Mike call my name from downstairs.

'They're coming up the path, love,' he said.

* * *

4

I had met Justin already, of course, just the previous Tuesday. In fact, it had only been a week since we'd been asked to consider our first placement at that point, and only eight days since I'd left my old job at the local comprehensive school. It had been an intense week, too, with everything seeming to move so quickly, and even though the way all these things were done was still new to us, Mike and I had both felt there was a real sense of desperation in the air. John Fulshaw, our link worker from the fostering agency we worked for, had been clear: this was not something we should undertake lightly. How little did we understand then just how true his words would be.

We'd been assigned John as our link worker when we'd first applied to be foster carers and we'd struck up a good relationship with him right away. By now we also felt we knew him quite well, so if John was anxious it naturally made me anxious too. Not that we weren't anticipating challenges. What Mike and I had signed up for wasn't mainstream fostering. It was an intense kind of fostering, intended to be short term in nature, which involved a new and complex programme of behaviour management. It had been trialled and was proving very successful in America, and had recently started to be funded by a number of councils in the UK. It was geared to the sort of kids who were considered unfosterable – the ones who had already been through the system and for whom the only other realistic future option was moving permanently into residential care. And not just ordinary residential care either – they'd usually already tried that – but, tragically, in secure units, many of these kids having already offended.

'The problem,' John had told me, during our first chat about Justin, 'is that we know so little about him and his past. And what we do know doesn't make for great reading, either. He's been in the care system since he was five and has already been through twenty failed placements. He's been through a number of foster families and children's homes, and now it's pretty much last chance saloon time. So what I'd like to do is to come round and discuss him with you both personally. Tomorrow, if it's not too short notice.'

As a family, we'd talked about that phone call all evening, trying to read anything and everything into John's few scraps of information about the child he wanted us to take on. What could the boy have done to end up having had twenty failed placements in just six short years? It seemed unfathomable. Just how damaged and unfosterable could he be? But since we knew almost nothing, it was pointless to speculate. We'd know all that soon enough, wouldn't we?

Not that, come morning, there was much more to know. John had arrived and, as soon as I'd made us all coffee, he got straight down to the business of telling us.

'It was a neighbour who alerted social services initially,' he explained. 'He'd been to their house several times, it seems, begging for food.'

We remained silent, while John sat and read from his notes. 'Family Support followed it up, by all accounts, but it seems the mother managed to convince them that she was coping okay – that she had just been through a bad patch at the time. Justin himself, it seems, corroborated this – certainly managing to convince them that the right course of action was to let things ride for a while. And then two months later, emergency services were called out to the family home by a neighbour. Seemed he'd been playing with some matches and burned the house down. Apparently the mother had left him and his two younger brothers –'

'Younger brothers? How old were they?' I asked him.

John checked his notes again. 'Let me see … two and three when it happened. And they'd all apparently been left alone in the house while she went off to visit a boyfriend. Seems the family dog died in the fire as well.'

Mike and I exchanged glances, but neither of us spoke. We could both see there was more for him to tell us.

John glanced at us both, then continued. 'It was after that that the mother agreed to have him taken into care. Under a voluntary care order – seems no fight was put up there about holding on to him; she was happy to let him go and accept a support package for the younger two – and he was placed in a children's home in Scotland, with contact twice monthly agreed. But it broke down after a year. It seems the people at the home felt they could do nothing for him. He was apparently' – he lowered his eyes to check on the exact wording – 'deemed angry, aggressive, something of a bully, and unable to make and keep friends. They felt he needed to be placed in a family situation for him to make any sort of progress.'

He leaned back in his chair then, while we took things in. The language used could have been describing an older child, certainly – an angry teenager, most definitely – but a five-year-old child? That seemed shocking to me. He was still just a baby.

'But he didn't,' I said finally.

John shook his head. 'No, sadly, he didn't. Because of his behaviour, he's been nowhere for more than a few months – no more than a few weeks, in some cases – since then. He's physically attacked several of his previous carers and has simply worn the rest of them out. So there we are,' he said, closing his file and straightening the papers within it. 'Twenty placements and we're all out of options.' He looked at both of us in turn now. 'So. What do you think?'

And now here I was, just a few days before Christmas, and this child, this 'unfosterable' eleven-year-old child who'd burned down his home at the tender age of just five, was about to become our responsibility.

I walked down the stairs just as I could see a shadow approaching in the glass of the front door. I noticed how smoothly my hand slid down the banister, and smiled. I'd been cleaning and polishing like a mad woman all morning, flicking my duster manically here, there and everywhere, and moving all sorts of stuff around the place. Mike, bless him, had been getting on my nerves since we'd got up, assuming, with his man-wisdom, that since I was obviously so stressed, that he'd be doing me a favour by anticipating my every next move, and being one step behind me at all times.

'Oh, for God's sake,' I'd snapped at him, not half an hour earlier. 'How can I get anything done in this place with you on my tail all the time?'

He'd shot off then, probably grateful to get out from under my feet. But he'd been right. I was so nervous that I actually felt physically sick. I'd never been so nervous about a new job, ever. Probably because this was going to *be* like no other new job. Because it wasn't just a job, it was a whole lifestyle. This was not nine till five, this was twenty-four-seven. Gone would be our cosy evenings in, cuddled on the sofa, just me and Mike together, and gone would be the lazy weekends we'd begun to start enjoying since Riley had moved out and Kieron had turned nineteen. There was no turning back, though. I'd said yes. I was committed. *He's only eleven*, I kept telling myself sternly. *He's been through some bad times*. It was just the lack of knowing *what* that was so worrying.

I reached the bottom of the staircase just as Mike reached the door. I took a deep breath. This was it, then.

'Hi Justin!' I said brightly as the door opened to reveal him, accompanied by Harrison Green, Justin's social worker, who'd brought him along for our initial meeting the previous Tuesday. I hadn't been sure about Harrison when I first met him; he seemed a scruffy sort of character to be a social worker, to my mind. In his mid-fifties, he had a mop of unruly, greying hair that looked like it hadn't seen a comb in a long while, and a generally unkempt air about him. But perhaps that was what long-term social work could do to you. I'd got little sense of what Justin himself was like on that occasion, other than that he was surly, a little awkward around us and a little lacking in all the normal social graces. Offered a biscuit, for example, and he'd immediately pounced on the plate, taking as many in one hand as he could get his fingers round, and immediately stashing half in his trouser pockets. But his lack of etiquette was hardly surprising given his situation, was it? So I wasn't concerned about such small, trifling details. Not at all. Those sorts of things could all be learned. It was the deeper stuff, the psychological damage, that most concerned me. Could the manifestations of that damage be *un*learned? That was what was key.

One thing that had happened was that we'd been given more background to chew over. While Mike had been showing Justin around our home that day, Harrison had taken the opportunity to fill me in on more of the details of his own.

'The truth is that he's attacked a number of his carers,' he'd told me gravely. 'With both fists and with kitchen knives, apparently.' He'd paused then. 'He's also threatened to take his life on a number of occasions, and did once actually try to hang himself. From some goalposts on the school playing fields.'

I'd listened in shock, mentally storing everything up so I could recount it all back to Mike later. It was then, too, that Harrison had passed on the news that Justin seemed to have a particular aversion to women with black hair. But he'd also been positive about the potential for his future progress. Justin's current situation had been as much to do with the carers as him, it seemed. According to Harrison, at any rate, they were too inexperienced to deal with Justin's refusal to accept boundaries. And boundaries were what he needed more than anything.

I'd not been convinced, at the time, that Harrison had really thought we'd be any better. He had a world-weary air about him that seemed to suggest otherwise. John's words about last-chance saloon came flooding back. Were Mike and I considered to be Justin's? Might our first placement be already doomed to failure?

I tried to dismiss the idea, telling myself I was being silly. We *were* last-chance-saloon fosterers – that was the whole point of the programme we were there to implement. But looking at Harrison now I sensed little had changed. That Harrison wasn't holding out a lot of hope, deep down. Just needed somewhere to place the child, and fast.

'Come on in,' Mike said warmly, standing aside to let them all enter. Justin did so with a fair degree of confidence compared with his last visit, I noticed, pulling Harrison along behind him into the living room.

'Is that all he's got?' I asked Harrison, following them, and gesturing to Justin's single battered suitcase. Yes it was big, but it still seemed very little in the scheme of things. Could it really contain all he had in the whole world?

'Um … er, yes,' Harrison replied, looking slightly flustered by my question. He seemed preoccupied with an agenda of his own.

And he was. 'I don't have much time, I'm afraid,' he told us. 'We're going to have to get the paperwork sorted out quickly, as I have to be somewhere else pretty soon … but you're alright,' he said, turning to Justin, who'd now sat down on the sofa. 'Looking forward to it, son, aren't you?'

Justin nodded, and managed to come up with a wonky half-smile. 'Is it okay if I put the telly on?' he asked me.

'Course,' I said, happy to see he really did seem okay, and so much more relaxed than he'd been with me last time. I smiled, feeling the tension drain away from me a little too. 'Just not too loud, though, okay?'

Harrison, on the other hand, was making me cross. 'Shall we go into the kitchen to complete the forms?' he asked me, visibly anxious to be making a move out through the door. It was as if he really couldn't wait to leave.

'Only one suitcase,' I persisted, as I led him through to the kitchen, while Mike went to show Justin how to work the TV remotes. 'I'd have thought a child who'd been in care as long as he has would have amassed loads and loads of stuff.' I did, too. This wasn't just whimsical thinking on my part. One of the things we'd covered during training was about kids in care and their various possessions. Kids coming straight from a bad home environment often have very little. Neglected and abused they often have owned very few things, and, in many cases, what little they do have tends to be hung on to by their families. Children already in care, on the other hand, *do* have possessions, often lots of them, because carers are given funds with which to buy them.

The Boy No One Loved

Harrison seemed irritated at being sidetracked from his paperwork. 'Yes, well,' he said, shuffling them. 'Justin doesn't really do "looking after things". Hence he travels light. So, then. Here are the care plans ...'

We went through them, and it was almost as if we were purchasing a car and he was the harried salesman handing us the log book, the deal done. I offered drinks but, no, he really *did* have to get away, and to be honest I was happy to see the back of him. His attitude towards the whole business of handing over Justin was getting up my nose every bit as much as his crumpled-up suit and musty smell.

Justin came into the kitchen immediately Harrison had left, his expression looking relaxed for the first time since we'd met. He was quite a stocky boy. Tall for his age, too. I'm five feet tall and he was only half a head shorter. He had thick, coarse blond hair, which seemed to grow upwards from his scalp, rather like a character in a cartoon who's just been electrocuted. And he was smiling now, which immediately softened his stony features. He wasn't an unattractive boy when he wasn't on his guard. One job, I mused, would be to work on that smile of his. And, hopefully, soon see much more of it.

'I'm glad he's gone,' he said to me, matter of factly. 'Is it nearly dinner time yet?'

I looked at the kitchen clock. It was only just coming up to eleven-thirty in the morning. 'Well,' I said. 'I suppose we could always have an early dinner, if you're hungry ...'

He shook his head 'Oh, I'm not. I just want to know what time we're having it,' he answered, in the same straightforward tone. 'Oh, and what we're having.'

'What we're having?'

Now he nodded at me. 'Yes.'

'Well,' I said, 'if you can hang on just for a little bit longer, I was going to phone my daughter Riley and my son Kieron – they're both *really* looking forward to meeting you, Justin. And we'll just be having a pasta bake, or something.'

'Twelve, then?' Now Justin did begin to look a bit flustered. 'And *will* it be pasta bake? Or might it be something else?'

'What was all that about?' asked Mike, once I'd reassured Justin that, yes, it would be twelve and it would definitely be pasta bake, and, satisfied now, he'd gone back to the living room. Mike chuckled. 'I'm surprised you didn't offer him a menu!'

It was good to hear my husband's familiar and reassuring words – the sound of sanity, the sound of normality. Probably just what this child needed in his life. But, just to be on the safe side I set to work on our unexpectedly early lunch anyway, while Mike went to call Kieron and Riley and tell them the coast was clear. We'd arranged for them to come only once Justin was safely with us, in order that we didn't overwhelm him.

As I chopped onions, I could hear Mike in the hall chuckling some more. 'Just make sure you ask for pasta!' he was telling them.

* * *

The Boy No One Loved

You'd be a fool as a foster carer, particularly our kind of foster carer, to let yourself be lulled into a false sense of security, but for a minute or two after Mike had finished talking to the kids, I felt hopeful that this would all work out well. Okay, so Justin seemed to have some anxieties about food, but then, after all those years in care and going from place to place, it would be strange if he *hadn't* picked up a few foibles along the way. I could see why food would have been something he'd possibly have to fight over in the different hierarchies of children and pubescents that existed in every new children's home he was billeted in.

But it wasn't the only foible he had, of course. I'd forgotten about the one we had already been warned about.

She's gorgeous, my daughter, and I love her to bits. She's welcoming and friendly, with a really bright personality, and had been so enthusiastic about the whole idea of us fostering. So when she and Kieron arrived she seemed as anxious as we were to make Justin feel like he belonged. When we were seated, the promised pasta bake steaming in the centre of the table, she sat down beside him and leaned towards him conspiratorially. 'Welcome to the mad house,' she said, grinning.

She then made a move, as if she was about to ruffle his hair, but even before she could lift up her hand to do so, Justin had slammed himself against his chair back and given her a really stony stare.

'Sorry, mate,' she said, shocked. 'I was just being friendly', but Justin ignored her, leaned forwards again and

15

Casey Watson

helped himself to a large portion of the pasta. I made a mental note that in future perhaps I'd need to serve the portions myself, in the kitchen.

We ate in an uncomfortable silence for some minutes, and I watched my daughter's face begin to redden. She was clearly so embarrassed and my heart really went out to her, and Mike, noticing too, tried to lighten the atmosphere by engaging the boys in conversation about football.

Justin wasn't interested, though, and continued to eat in silence, a silence becoming more noisy and intrusive by the minute as we all digested what had happened.

'Is David coming round?' I asked Riley eventually.

'No,' she said, shaking her head. 'Not till tomorrow. He's working today …' She tailed off because Justin was staring at her once again. 'David's my boyfriend,' she explained to him. 'We live just round the corner. He's looking forward to meeting you, too, Justin.'

But once again it seemed Riley was the devil incarnate. 'What time is tea, Casey?' he asked me, ignoring her. 'And what are we having to eat?'

I could feel Mike begin to bristle beside me. 'Justin, Riley was speaking to you, mate,' he said quietly. 'And we don't know about tea yet. We're only just having dinner.'

'It's okay, Dad,' Riley said. 'It's fine. It really is. I'm always quiet around people I don't know too.'

Justin scowled at her and once again turned to face me. 'Is it okay if I take my stuff to my room now?'

'Go ahead,' said Mike. 'I'll come up and check on you in a bit.'

16

'Oh, my God! How rude is that kid?' Kieron observed, once we'd heard Justin's tread on the stairs. My lovely Kieron, who finds it impossible to see bad in anybody. He looked at his elder sister. 'He sure doesn't seem to like you, Riley!'

Riley frowned. 'It's probably just because of my black hair.'

'Your black hair? Why?'

She glanced in my direction. 'Mum told me. He's got this thing, apparently. Has this thing about hating women with black hair.'

Kieron glanced at me too, looking shocked. The word 'hate' didn't really exist for him. 'I know,' I said, having completely forgotten all about that. Of course! 'But we've also got to remember this is probably a bit too much for him. We have to be patient and give him a chance to settle in.'

Mike got up and began clearing the plates. He was shaking his head as he went out to the kitchen.

While Mike manfully tackled the washing up, I went outside with Riley for a cigarette. I'd been trying to cut down, in preparation for giving up, but right now I really needed a quick nicotine boost. I reassured my daughter that things could only improve; that it would take time, but that once we got to know Justin a little better it would all become easier and less stressful for us all.

She didn't look convinced – Riley was someone who liked to be liked and I could see that, even though she understood about the black-hair thing, she was still shocked and confused by Justin's very obvious rejection of her – so I just hoped what I was saying would turn out to be true.

I could still hear plenty of banging and clattering in the kitchen, so I accepted a sneaky second cigarette, feeling the strain of the morning start to ebb away. Justin's food issues, at least, were something we could definitely address, and as for his thing about black hair – well, I was sure once he got to know us as real people, that would lessen too.

I was just stubbing out the cigarette when Kieron came to the back door to find me.

'Mum!' he said, looking shocked. 'You have to come!'

I started. 'Come where? What's the matter?'

'Dad's just been up to check on Justin and …' He seemed completely stuck for words. 'And his room is … well …' He frowned at me, looking anxious. 'Come on. Just come up and see for yourself.'

Chapter 2

I followed Kieron up the stairs, Riley close behind me, wondering what on earth could have happened. We turned the corner of the landing to see Mike standing speechless in the doorway to Justin's bedroom. He moved out of the way so Riley and I could look into the room.

It was almost unrecognisable, and I really couldn't take it in. The lovely room I'd so carefully prepared for Justin's arrival over several days – the place I'd planned so minutely so it would feel welcoming and homely and a safe place of refuge – now looked exactly like a prison cell. There was a long, low cupboard, with some drawers in, under the window, which I had covered with a set of books, a few football figurines, some jigsaw puzzles and a craft box I'd found for him, which contained glue, felt and fabric, sticky paper and gummed stars. Now every one of these items had been hidden out of sight – I couldn't even work out where he'd put them. The bookcase had been similarly dealt with. I was so shocked, for this had been in some ways the room's centrepiece; we'd painted it ourselves, in a pattern of red and white blocks, and glued on lots of black and white paper footballs. We'd then filled it with yet more things we thought he'd like – more books, some soft toys, pens and pencils and so on. But it too had now disappeared. He'd covered the whole thing by draping it completely with the blue fleece throw I had bought for the bed. The round football rug had been removed and, I presumed, hidden – I certainly couldn't see it – and the array of fluffy cushions had disappeared from the bed. He'd also closed the curtains so the room was in darkness, making it feel really gloomy and depressing.

In the middle of all this sat Justin, on the bed. He had his knees pulled up close to his chest, and was playing on a hand-held computer game he had resting against them; one that he'd obviously brought with him. Most compelling about the scene though was that he seemed completely indifferent to us all crowded there, open mouthed, in the doorway, and just carried on playing the game, his face partly obscured by the controller, his fingers flying over the controls.

'Justin,' I gasped at him. 'What have you done to your room, love?' I waited, but he didn't answer. Didn't even look up. 'Hey, love,' I persisted. 'Where's everything gone?'

Now he calmly moved the console enough so that I could see his whole face. 'It's my room, innit?' he answered coldly. 'And this is how I like it.'

It was then that I properly noticed that not everything had gone. He might have stripped the room, but there were two notable exceptions. The TV and DVD player hadn't been banished. So it wasn't a case of *total*, self-imposed deprivation, then.

It was that – that one very specific omission from what he'd done – that made me cross. In fact, all at once, it made me really upset. I'd spent hours agonising over that bloody room and days and days shopping for it and decorating it and everything. And for what? Just to have it trashed by this smug-faced, overweight and downright rude eleven-year-old. It made me see red. I wasn't happy at all.

Mike, perhaps sensing this, placed a hand lightly on my shoulder and ushered me gently back out to the landing, signalling at the same time for Kieron and Riley to go back downstairs. 'Right, Justin,' he said mildly, 'you just come down when you're ready, okay? Or if you need anything …'

I was even more furious, hearing Mike say that. I marched back down the stairs and stomped into the kitchen, rounding on Mike as he followed me in there. '"If he needs anything!"' I jabbed a finger towards the ceiling. 'Have you seen that bloody room up there?' I just couldn't take it in. I spread my palms in exasperation. 'Why would he *do* that?'

I could see the kids braced a little, in readiness for the rant they could see I was building up to. 'I can't believe it, Mike!' I fumed. 'I really can't! The ungrateful little …'

'Casey!' Mike had raised his voice to my level now. 'Let's not forget what we're dealing with here!' He looked hard at me. 'And let's try to remember where's he's come from, okay? For God's sake, love, If he were Little Lord Fauntleroy, he wouldn't be in bleeding care, now, would he?'

I could still see the kids, out of the corner of my eye, now stifling giggles at their father's analogy. And suddenly, I felt all my anger drain away – almost as quickly and completely as it had come. I started laughing, and the kids did as well, laughing harder and harder, till the tears began streaming down all of our cheeks. It was one of those surreal situations where you really think you're going to cry and the next you find you're laughing hysterically. There would be many more laugh-or-you'll-cry situations down the line, but right now I didn't know that. All I knew was that we'd crossed some sort of threshold; that, as a family, we were in completely new territory.

Mike wasn't laughing. In fact, quite the opposite. He was looking at the three of us as if we'd all gone completely mad. 'Sorry, love,' I spluttered at him. 'It's *so* not funny, I know that. But I can't help it. Really, I can't.'

His face softened a bit then. 'I know,' he said, nodding towards upstairs. 'But maybe pipe down just a little, eh? We don't want him to hear us and think we're all laughing at his expense, do we? I don't think that would help the situation any. Do you?'

'You're right,' I said, pulling myself together with an effort. 'Come on, kids, pipe down, like Dad says.' And, bless them, they duly did.

'You know what I think?' suggested Riley, crossing the kitchen and reaching for the kettle. 'I wonder if he's determined not to enjoy his time with us, and him doing what he did to his bedroom is his way of sort of making the point.'

Mike nodded. 'I think you might have hit the nail on the head there,' he agreed. 'And I also wonder – given what we *do* know about him – if he's so used to having his possessions taken away from him for bad behaviour that he prefers not to get attached to any in the first place?'

I walked across to join Riley and get some mugs down from the cupboard. 'Well, whatever the reason,' I said. 'It's strange. And so sad.' I shook my head and glanced across at Mike. 'And I think this is going to be a lot harder than we expected.'

My family's temporary silence spoke volumes. I'd been right. We all knew it. This *was* going to be hard. Not necessarily the day-to-day looking after the child – I could do all that with my eyes shut. It was just the impact of having this small stranger living with us, among us. One who we didn't understand. *That* was hard.

I of all people should really have known what we'd gotten into. It had been barely two weeks since I'd left my last job, even though it suddenly felt a lifetime ago. And prior to that job I had worked in a huge organisation, running self-development courses for disadvantaged teens. Young people who teetered on the edge of society for various reasons, helping them to take some control over their lives and to make positive changes to empower them. I had spent the last three years of my working life as a behaviour manager at our huge local secondary school, running the unit for children with behavioural difficulties. These were the sort of children that almost every school has, sadly. The ones that just don't fit in well, for a whole host of reasons. The ones that disrupt classes, taunt teachers, cause problems for themselves and everyone else. The sort of children, in consequence, that everybody wants to pass on to someone else. And I'd loved it, loved pretty much every minute of it, actually. I loved that I could do something positive for the sort of kids whose home lives were so tough that school was often their only safe haven, which made it doubly important that they could be helped to stay there. Because the bottom line was that if it weren't for units such as the one I'd worked in, these were the children who were most likely to end up excluded altogether – which would be the worst outcome of all for them.

But it was doing that – connecting with these sorts of children – that had, by chance, led me to this whole new career choice. When I'd started at the school, my job had been reasonably straightforward: I'd be responsible for two or three children at a time, whom I'd supervise from my own office. With only a small number of children, I could really get through to them. And more often than not, I found, it was this close relationship – this one-on-one attention – that really made the difference in their behaviour. Away from their peers and the demands and anxieties of the classroom, they would often open up with me about their problems. My favourite thing of all was to take them to McDonald's. There was something about sitting in a fast-food restaurant, over a burger, that seemed to help make them slow down, take stock and, most of all, trust me – enough to let me really try to help them.

But life being what it is, and budgets being budgets, my job had started growing at an incredible rate. By the time of my leaving, I had fifty children on my list, and had had to take over a classroom in which to house them – one that was swiftly re-christened 'The Unit'. Here, the children would be divided into three distinct groups: the ones who were generally disruptive and uncooperative; the ones who tended to be bullied and friendless; and then the third group – the ones I classed as being the 'unknown quantities'. These were the really sad, quiet kids. The ones who wouldn't or couldn't participate or interact. These were the obvious victims of poverty or neglect, and it really impacted on their learning.

It was a big job, and I had the use of teaching assistants when they were available, but, as is the case in most schools, they very seldom were, being in chronically short supply. Instead, I would often have to ask volunteer sixth-form students if they'd come along and give me a hand. Then, together with whatever willing helpers I could get, I'd work with each group separately throughout the day.

The day itself could throw up all sorts of challenges. I might start by seeing a group of kids that were targets for bullies, sitting with them and discussing ways in which they could build up their self-esteem; we'd also look at what action they should take if they found themselves in a vulnerable situation. These kids seemed to thrive best when we did team-building activities or they were given responsibilities around the school.

Next, I might have a group of kids that were known to *be* bullies; these, in contrast, I would talk to about the results of their actions and the impact they had on the kids they bullied. I did a lot of empathy work with these kinds of students, and tried to get them to really understand the emotional damage they caused. Usually, I found that the bullies had unresolved problems of their own, and when this was the case we were very proactive, with both extra support and interventions being put in place.

As time went on, I'd also begun spending more and more time working with some of the parents, as well, in a kind of unofficial 'super-nanny' capacity. This increasingly meant doing home visits, sometimes well into the evening, which was well outside my contracted professional respon- sibilities – not to mention time-consuming – and so was becoming a bit draining in itself.

All in all, my 'unit' had fast become the victim of its own success. The school community is like any other – if some- thing's happening, good or bad, word quickly spreads. And, in this case, it was a regular topic of conversation in the staff room, with all the teachers agreeing how much more pleasant life had become since this disruptive child or that disruptive child was regularly removed from their lessons. As a consequence, new teachers were regularly accosting me and, me being a softie, I could never say no.

It became increasingly difficult, therefore, to help *any* of the kids in the way I really wanted to help them, and little by little it began to become obvious to me that helping lots of children, just a little, here and there, wasn't the best use of my time or experience. Wouldn't it be better to concentrate on making a real difference by helping one child at a time, but in a *big* way?

And it wasn't just this that had led Mike and I to fostering. We had already had hands-on experience of the realities of challenging parenting because Kieron had a mild form of Asperger's syndrome, which meant he was just a little different from other kids.

Kieron was gorgeous on the outside (a slim six-foot blond Adonis – and he knew it!) but, more importantly, he was gorgeous on the inside as well. He really didn't seem to have a bad bone in his body, and had never had an enemy in his life. It may have been a part of his condition – we both felt so – but Kieron really didn't understand unpleasantness or malice, and could only see the good in every single person he ever met. He also had a great love for animals.

But his condition also meant he had to live life a certain way. He had to have a plan worked out for everything – still does – and really hated it if anything was changed at the eleventh hour. If we were going to do something, or had planned some sort of outing, woe betide us if we tried to change things at the last minute because sudden change really upset him and made him anxious. As a young child, this distress was very obvious to witness. He'd grow jumpy and panicky and be obviously unhappy. He'd also chew away all the skin around his fingers, leaving his hands really painful and raw. As a teenager, and still now, as a young adult, if he was upset he would simply stop speaking and begin to withdraw. Even now, though, if things got really on top of him, he'd still exhibit obvious signs of discomfort and distress, which, being his mum, I was always tuned into.

He was also, like many kids with Asperger's syndrome, a passionate cataloguer and collector. His bedroom was always a sight to behold as he had collections of anything and everything. Football figurines and programmes, photographs of celebrities, classic cars, autographs, personal memorabilia … All the birthday cards he'd ever been given in his life, for instance, were all catalogued in a neat and perfect order. His DVDs were all ordered by favourite actors, and so on, his cars by colour, his music CDs by artist. And, naturally, you messed with any of it at your peril.

It was Kieron, more than anything, that gave us pause for thought when we seriously started thinking about training for fostering. At 19 he was an adult, but still a vulnerable adult, and as he lived at home we both had to think really hard about the impact our plans might have on him because our plans were not just to foster children. While researching 'working with difficult children' on the internet, as I'd started doing when I'd become restless about the growing problems of my job, I followed a link through to this new and quite specific kind of fostering, which had been successful in trials in America, where it had first been developed. It used a behaviour-modification model, based on accruing points for good behaviour, in which we'd both be fully trained, and which was specifically geared to help the most difficult children, the ones unsuited to main-stream foster placements. These were the sort of children for whom life was pretty bleak – the sort of children I was well used to dealing with in school, and whom I knew I was in a position to best help. *This* was the type of fostering that really excited me, and once I'd found out all about it, I was hooked.

I lay in bed that night, my ears straining for signs of activity in Justin's bedroom, feeling sleepless and weighed down by worry. For all the training we'd received – six intense months of it, and so much preparation and expectation – I don't think either Mike or I had really been prepared for the massive impact of having this child enter our lives. He wasn't only hostile, he was also a completely unknown quantity, and here he was, feet away, sleeping under our roof, having turned my whole family upside down in less than twenty-four hours. Only one thing felt certain as I finally drifted off. We were now committed. There was no going back.

Chapter 3

I'm mad about Christmas – always have been and always will be – and usually start my Christmas planning way ahead. By December, of course, it's generally all falling into place – so since at least two weeks before Justin's arrival in the family, I'd already started my usual Run Up To The Big Day.

We lived in a comfy four-bed semi, with a large back garden, in a small village on the outskirts of a big town. It was the sort of tight-knit community where everyone knew everyone else and it's probably fair to say that the Watson household was something of a landmark at this time of year. I was never much of a one for gardening – bar a few pots of flowers I kept clustered around my back door – but come Christmas I was like a woman possessed. I loved this time of year and I didn't care who knew it. My Christmas tree was already up and twinkling gaily – Riley had wittily remarked that it looked like a fairy had thrown up on it (she's such a wag, my daughter) – and I had festooned fairy lights and decorations pretty much everywhere else. Outside, I'd continued to indulge my obsession by putting up an inflatable Santa, another tree with flashing lights, plus a neon reindeer complete with a present-laden sleigh. I'd also found some more fairy lights to drape over the front hedge, and the net result was that, entirely as usual, my house looked the tackiest on the street.

What Justin thought of all this, I didn't know. It was naive of me, perhaps, given the wealth of my experience with troubled kids, but I think I just got carried away with making everything super special for him – to try and show him how family life *could* be. One of the things that was uppermost in my mind was that on Boxing Day Justin had an important visit to make. Mike was to drive him for a few hours to where his mother and young brothers now lived. It was to be an overnight visit – his first, we'd been told, since around three months before we'd met him; around the time she'd apparently got herself a new boyfriend.

We knew so little about it all, but what we did know was that such visits were sporadic, at best, and appeared to always coincide with new boyfriends. She tended to want to see him whenever she hooked up with a new one, only to drop him again as soon as he'd served his purpose; to show her as being sufficiently 'motherly'. It was heart-breaking stuff, even in the telling. How could she do that to her own child? How could any mother treat her flesh and blood in that way? I knew the pressure of it must have been hanging over Justin. After my small outburst on the night of his arrival, I had got my head back together and was beginning to feel more positive about Justin again. Though schools were now closed for the holidays, I'd been able to get in touch with the local education authority and had secured a place for him in our local secondary, so he could start straight away in the new year. It was handy that I'd previously worked there, of course, as I already had a good relationship with the head and the support staff; something I had an inkling might come in very useful now we were fostering the kind of children that would probably need them. Also, because the papers showed that his educational level had fallen so far behind the norm, he'd been given an ELAC (Education for Looked After Children) worker, who was called Helen King, and who seemed really nice. She'd also allocated a school budget for an extra learning support worker for him so he could get the help he needed to catch up – something I could have done with back in my unit, for sure.

So it was all shaping up well, and though Justin's food anxieties needed addressing in the short term (I'd now, at his request, put up a chart in the kitchen, detailing exactly what food we were having each day, and at what time) he seemed to be slowly settling in. Though he seemed to oscillate between being over-excited about Christmas one minute and negative and scowling about the whole thing the next, I felt overall that we were making progress. So much so that, at the end of the week, I felt confident enough to take him out on a Christmas shopping trip, with me and Riley.

'How big is big?' he asked me, as our train to the shopping mall sped through the snowy countryside. He'd been chatty and in good spirits and had been animated throughout the journey. He told us he'd never been to a big city-centre shopping mall before.

'Big,' I said. 'Lots and lots of shops. Around fifty of them, most probably.'

This news seemed to enthral him. 'And will they have a Christmas tree?' he asked.

'Definitely,' I said, grinning. 'Several of them. Really big ones, I expect, with loads of lights and baubles.'

He seemed pleased at this, too, even though I recalled that his last comment about our one had been that my 'stupid fucking fairy lights' gave him a migraine. Today, though, was definitely an 'up' day. So far, so good.

'I want DVDs for Christmas,' he went on, at Riley's cheerful prompting about what Santa might be bringing him. 'I'd like lots of DVDs to watch, and a new games console and lots of games. And some plastic toy soldiers that I can play with in the bath.' Riley raised her eyebrows slightly, her meaning immediately obvious. Wasn't he just a little old to be playing with toy soldiers in the bath?

I nodded anyway. He might have had to grow up way, way too fast in some respects, but in others, understandably, given his life experiences, he'd probably still be very immature. 'And what else, besides soldiers?' I asked him.

'Toy guns,' he said. 'Toy guns and a Swiss army knife.'

From one end of the spectrum to the other. 'I think you're still a little bit too young for one of those,' I told him gently. 'Perhaps when you're a little older …'

But the change in Justin as I said this was both immediate and dramatic. Thwarted, his mouth narrowed straight away into a thin angry line, his eyes darkened and his whole face was now set in a scowl. He refused to engage with either of us for the remainder of the journey. And there was absolutely nothing either of us could do about it.

Once we arrived, however, it seemed Justin was once again too excited to be angry with us any more, and looked up in wonder at the decorations, the shop fronts and the huge crowds of people. He seemed particularly ecstatic about the food court on the top floor, and the fact that there were so many different fast-food places you could choose to eat from. Paradoxically, however – and it felt I was learning all this far too slowly – he got really upset again when I suggested he might like to be the one who chose where we'd have lunch.

'It's not fair, Casey!' he railed at me. He was unnervingly articulate and seemed palpably distressed again. 'You know I love *all* these places! You shouldn't have brought us here if you can't make your mind up about it. I feel sick now, and it's *all your fault*!'

I quickly chose one, and we diffused things, and lunch happened fairly peaceably but a similar thing happened when we started going round the shops. We were given a specific allowance for Justin by our fostering agency, which we could give to him as pocket money, and I'd brought along thirty pounds for him to buy presents for his mother and two little brothers.

Not wishing to smother him or seem prescriptive over what would be personal choices, I then sent him into a shop alone, while Riley and I waited outside. He was gone a long time, and when he did finally emerge, empty handed, I could see that the dark expression had overtaken him again.

'It's shit in there!' he shouted, as he stormed across the concourse to where we were sitting. 'There's too much in there. I don't know what to buy!' He then turned to Riley, and I could see he was close to tears now. 'Please,' he said to her, 'can you choose for me?'

'Of course,' she said, leaping up, and leading him straight back inside again. They returned minutes later and his face was much brighter. They'd got a necklace for his mum and two superhero models for his brothers, and he seemed genuinely pleased to have had her help him. And as we left the mall, it occurred to me that his see-saw behaviour was, in fact, very understandable. Was there anything more difficult for children who had nothing – and more than that, no-one to love them or to care for them – than seeing a world full of families and so much festive cheer and joy? It was particularly hard, given his desperate and lonely situation, and the fact that he was going to be 'allowed' to see his mother for just a few hours in as many long months.

But there was also a big positive in all this, I reflected. He seemed to have at least got over his animosity towards Riley. So, on balance, a very productive day.

* * *

As Christmas Day itself – the Big One – loomed ever nearer, Justin also found an unlikely ally in Kieron. Though Justin was still intermittently excited about everything, the strain on all of us was showing because for the most part his mood, with the endless waves of friends and relatives stopping by, and all the attendant disruption and chatter, was becoming more volatile and darker with every passing hour.

And we did have an awful lot of visitors. My brother and his family stayed over, and we had lots dropping in, from neighbours to friends to some of my old colleagues from school. The house was constantly full of noise – good noise, in the main; lots of fun and lots of laughter – but Justin increasingly sought to avoid it or, if he did stick around, seemed intent on embarrassing me, telling my niece and nephew that there was no such thing as Santa, swearing, slamming doors and drowning out any conversation by pointedly turning the volume on the TV to max. But it was me, as it turned out, that needed teaching a lesson, and it was through Kieron, my own son, that I got one.

Much as he loved Christmas, Kieron found it stressful too, as it obviously meant major changes to his routine, and lots of unscheduled comings and goings, which always made him nervous. He would often, therefore, take off to his bedroom the minute he heard the sound of the doorbell.

On the day of my brother's visit, my little niece, Brooke, wanted to give Kieron his present herself, but when I looked for him I realized couldn't find him. When I'd last seen him he'd been in the conservatory, putting up some last-minute decorations for me, but when I called him I got no response. I ran upstairs, planning to pop my head round his bedroom door, but as I approached I could hear male voices and laughter coming from Justin's room. I stopped outside then, and heard Kieron's voice. 'I know how you feel, mate. Mum's always like this,' he was saying. I realized immediately that he must be talking to Justin. 'She's always been like it,' he mused. 'She just loves all the noise and having loads of people round.' I heard him laugh then. 'Trouble is, she thinks everyone else does as well!'

Then Justin spoke. 'That's okay,' he said. 'You can stay here with me, if you like. Stay in my room till everyone's gone, if you want to. We can play footie manager – as long as I can be Germany. Okay? You can be England, and we'll kick your butt.'

'Set it up, then,' Kieron replied, laughing. 'Let's see how good you *really* are.'

I crept away then, the idea of calling Kieron down now off the agenda, and cursing myself for being so lacking in perspective that I couldn't see that not everyone was as Christmas crazy as I was. God, it was *my* butt that needed kicking.

And, of course, I did get my comeuppance, because it duly got kicked. By Christmas Eve, despite my determination to be mindful of how hyper I could get at this time of year, I was in overdrive. Christmas Eve was always a busy day for me anyway but this one was even busier than usual. Not least because I was up so early – before Justin got up – ringing round all my friends and family to explain that we'd decided to cancel our planned Christmas Eve party. Mike and I had discussed it at length and decided it was the only sensible thing to do; we just didn't think Justin would be able to cope with it.

Kieron was pleased, but poor Riley was not. 'God, Mum!' she launched at me, in an uncharacteristic outburst. 'That kid is beginning to ruin everything already! David and I were both really looking forward to tonight. And now it's going to be crap. Thanks a lot.'

'I'm sorry,' I began, 'but –'

'And why does he have to be here anyway?' she interrupted. 'Surely there's *someone* who wants to see him over Christmas? Why can't you just sort it so he can go somewhere else tonight?'

I tried to explain gently to her that, really, there was no-one, and to suggest that perhaps she was being just a little selfish; that the whole point of us fostering was to help this unhappy child. We'd hardly be doing that if we packed him off at any time, but to do so at Christmas – how could we?

To my great relief (tinged with guilt; this was her mum and dad's choice, after all, not hers) she accepted this and came over to help me wrap some presents, while Kieron and Justin played yet more Football Manager upstairs. I'd dispatched Mike, meanwhile (and not at all to his liking) to head to town with my last-minute shopping list.

The Boy No One Loved

Perhaps, I thought, just perhaps, all would be well. I took a deep breath. So far, at least.

But the calm in the Watson household wasn't destined to last. It was around four in the afternoon and by now I was busy in the kitchen, preparing the veg for our Christmas dinner the next day. Justin had been downstairs a couple of times, moaning about how I hadn't written what we were having for tea on the chart yet, and when he made a third appearance, I was short with him.

'Look, love,' I said to him, conscious even then that I was irritable. 'I am trying to get the food ready for tomorrow. I do have other things on my mind besides what you're having for your tea!'

Almost as soon as I'd said this, I wished I could have swallowed the words, because Justin's reaction was instantaneous. His eyes darkened, in that rather scary way we'd come to witness – a sure sign that he'd lost it, and big time.

'You can stick your tea and your Christmas up your arse!' he roared at me, before flying from the room and slamming the kitchen door so hard I was sure it made the walls rattle.

Kieron appeared in the kitchen moments later, presumably having heard this and passed Justin on the stairs. I tried to bite back the tears that were springing from my eyes. I don't think until that moment I'd really accepted quite how stressed out I really was, and the last thing I wanted was for Kieron to see it now. But within seconds, things were about to get worse. Before I had even started telling Kieron what had just occurred, Justin burst back in through the door, his eyes now blazing, his cheeks florid,

39

brandishing all the Disney DVDs that we'd bought for him, screaming manically as he snapped them, one by one, in half.

'This is what I think of your stupid fucking tea!' he screamed at me. 'And this is what I think of your stupid fucking presents! They're for kids!' he yelled, as shards of DVD flew across the kitchen. 'So why don't you give them to your ugly fucking niece! I don't want them, okay? And I couldn't play them anyway! Because I've smashed up my DVD player, too!'

'Justin –' I began.

But Justin was unseeing, and not listening to me at all. He grabbed my mobile from the kitchen table and hurled it against the wall. The back flew off immediately and the battery fell out, the bits joining the mass of DVD shards. It was so sudden that it took me completely by surprise, and I just stood there and gaped for a moment, speechless.

'Get to your room! NOW!' Kieron suddenly barked at him. 'And don't even think about coming down until you're ready to apologise! You're a selfish little brat, and if it were up to me, you'd be having no tea at *all*, you understand?'

Justin's eyes were now as full of unshed tears as my own were, and as he fled the room, mine spilled out over my cheeks, despite all my good intentions about not crying.

I pulled out a chair and sat on it and put my head in my hands, mortified both that I'd handled things so badly, and that I'd upset Kieron. Upset everything. Ruined Christmas.

But I didn't sit on it for long. What was I *thinking*? I stood up again, and went to put my arm around Kieron, as he stooped to gather up the parts of my dismembered phone. He was white as a sheet and I could feel he was shaking.

'It's okay, love,' I soothed him. He hated seeing me upset. 'He probably just needed to get that out of his system. I think we all did. I'm okay, Kieron, honest.'

'Oh, God, mum. I know. But, *God*, I almost *slapped* him!' This thought clearly horrified him, as I knew it would. That wasn't Kieron. He looked hard at me. 'Are you sure you're okay?'

I squeezed his shoulder. 'I'm fine now. Really fine. I *swear*.'

I took a step back from him now, gently shaking his shoulders. 'But look at you! Coming over all Bruce Lee for your mum!'

He tutted at this. 'Bruce Lee? He's *ancient*! Bruce Willis, more like.'

Whatever. I let go a big sigh of relief. Situation diffused. At least for now.

By the time Mike returned with the shopping, I had calmed down sufficiently to see clearly. This was just an outburst – a symptom – not the end of the word. Kieron, understandably, was still very angry and insistent that Justin come and apologize to me, but after he'd explained to Mike what had happened, I felt it was really important that we calm the whole temperature down. I neither wanted nor needed an apology, I told them. It was just the build-up, the anticipation; it had all clearly been too much for him. I should have thought, I went on, about how it must be for him. How different it must have all been from what he was used to. And despite us telling him that Santa was bringing him lots of presents, why should he believe us? He hadn't seen them, because we'd hidden them. And why, with his past, should he trust any of us? Trust anyone?

Despite that, Mike still felt he must go up and speak to him. Not to rant at him – that, we both agreed, would be pointless; even counter-productive. He was probably well used to people tearing strips off him all the time – but just to make it clear that his behaviour was unacceptable. He already knew that, of course – he'd know he'd lose points on his behaviour chart – but Mike felt strongly that he needed not to gloss over it, but to spell it out.

They both came back down, half an hour later, and Justin's head was hanging. His eyes were red and swollen. You could see he'd been crying a lot.

'I'm sorry Casey,' he said solemnly. 'I'm sorry, Kieron. I'll pay you back for everything with my pocket money, I promise. I've got £16 in my drawer too, so that'll be a start.'

He looked so sorry and so ashamed that my heart melted instantly. Poor kid. Poor, poor kid. Born to such terrible circumstances, and none of it his fault.

'Just forget it,' I said to him. But Mike shook his head.

'No, Casey,' he said. 'We've already sorted it, haven't we, Justin? That we'll get him a new DVD player once he's saved up enough to pay half. Agreed, Justin?'

Justin nodded. 'Agreed.'

I crossed the kitchen and ruffled Justin's hair. And he let me. It was only a small thing, but at least we'd made some contact.

Once again, I felt the tension drain out of my body, and my sense of optimism about Christmas returning. It would be fine now. Outburst over, we could now all enjoy Christmas and New Year.

But it would be less than forty-eight hours before I was proved wrong.

Chapter 4

I woke on Christmas morning in my usual good spirits, and was once again up early, and straight down in the living room, flicking through the TV channels to find something festive to put on. After a few clicks of the remote I found *The Wizard of Oz* – one of my favourites – so I left that playing while I headed into the kitchen to prepare breakfast, where I added my Christmas CD to the cacophony, turning it up just that little bit too much.

'For God's sake, love!' said Mike, following me in there in his dressing gown.

I pulled him towards me and tried to get him to do a twirl with me, but he was having none of it. 'Get off me, you nutter!' he said, grinning. 'You'll have the whole bloody street up with the racket you're making! Go get some breakfast on, woman!'

He then kissed me on the nose and gave me a bear hug. 'I'll go and get these kids up, then, shall I?'

I smiled to myself as I went to the fridge and started pulling out bacon and orange juice. I had the best husband ever. I truly believed that. Never in a million years would I have considered becoming a foster parent if I hadn't had a great man like Mike by my side.

By the time we took on Justin, Mike and I had been married for twelve years, though we had been together as a couple for much longer. We'd known each other since childhood, and had always been friends. It was only after my first marriage had broken down and I had turned to friends for support, that Mike and I had realised just how much we meant to each other. The rest, as they say, is history, and we remain just as much in love today as we always were.

He was also my rock and my foil – we fitted perfectly. Where I was impetuous and excitable, he was so calm and wise, and he also made me feel safe, both emotionally and physically – he was well over six foot to my diminutive five foot nothing, and I knew I could rely on him totally.

I glanced at the many reminders and post-it notes stuck on the fridge door as I closed it, and which I'd had to prune out and squash up to make way for some big new ones. Beside the meal chart – on which I'd remembered to record both our turkey dinner *and* our bacon buttie breakfast – was the points chart we'd had in place for Justin from day one, as part of our strategy to get him to modify his behaviour and so – hopefully – be in a position to return to mainstream foster care once he'd completed the programme with us. That was all that we were hoping for (though the word 'all' is obviously a pretty big one) – to get him success-fully placed with a long-term foster family and thereby have a chance of a happy and useful adult life.

The way we worked the points chart was simple. When he had amassed sufficient he was allowed a choice of treats as a reward; things like choosing the family dinner, say, or having an outing of some sort, the hope being that he'd be motivated to try and earn them. Because no points, of course, meant no treats. If he was good, and did all the day-to-day things we required of him, like cleaning his teeth, making his bed, being polite and so on, he got points awarded. But if he did something bad, he would lose them again. Last night's episode, sadly, had seen him lose a lot. But, largely thanks to Mike's input, he'd apologised now, which was no small thing for a child in his situation to do. I was so glad we were now starting Christmas Day on a positive note. The only fly in the ointment was an obvious one. We'd bought him some DVDs for Christmas, as had Riley, and a few others, and now he had nothing on which to play them.

But there was no point in me worrying about that now. We'd just have to deal with it when we got to it, I supposed. At the moment all was calm and that was good enough for me.

And also Kieron, who was down in the kitchen moments later, clearly back to his old self after the scene he had witnessed last night, and as excited about Christmas at 19 years of age as he'd been throughout the whole of his child-hood. Where the run-up meant stress and anxiety and disruption, the big day itself was completely predictable, being one of those days in the calendar where our family routine hardly varied, which meant it was perfect for someone like my son. Mostly, of course, it meant lots of presents, which we still – at his request – put into a great big Christmas sack.

We'd done one for Justin, too, who thundered down close behind Kieron, looking so much calmer and happier now the day itself was finally here. In some respects, they had quite a lot in common.

I tried keeping some order on proceedings in the living room, but it was pointless. Since we'd had children big enough to create chaos, it always had been. 'Check the tags, love,' I urged Justin, as he ripped hell for leather into all the wrapping paper, 'or you won't have any idea who bought you what!'

My words were falling on deaf ears, though; he was just way too excited to take heed of what I was saying, and I decided that since this was probably a really big deal for him, I wouldn't spoil the moment by nagging. 'Tell you what,' I said, as I stooped to gather up all the discarded wrapping paper, 'you'll just have to say "thank you for my present" to everyone. That way you won't go far wrong.'

I was so touched by what an impressive haul he had, too. Everyone in my extended family had got him something, which they really didn't have to do, bless them. I was particularly touched to see how much care Riley had taken. This was a child she'd not laid eyes on till half-way through December, not to mention the fact that she and David didn't exactly have fortunes to splash around, yet she'd bought him such a lovely collection of toy soldiers, together with all the guns and grenades and other bits and bobs to go with them. I found myself smiling at this, too – we'd be having a job getting him out of the bath now.

The floor of the lounge was by now a sea of presents and torn paper, and it was the rustling of this that made me turn to see Mike sloping out. I'd assumed he'd just gone out to turn over the bacon, but he returned with a present I'd not seen before. He handed it to a surprised-looking Justin.

'You might need this,' he said, grinning, and before I could even wonder, Justin had opened the package to find a DVD player inside. He whispered a shocked but clearly delighted 'thank you' to Mike, and the expression on his face – now rather red – was a picture. As, I'm sure, was the expression on mine.

'Where on earth did that come from?' I asked Mike once we were back alone in the kitchen, getting breakfast dished up.

'I called our Angela last night, after you'd gone up to bed,' he explained. Angela was his sister. 'I just kept thinking we couldn't have the lad with nothing to play his new DVDs on, could we? I mean, I know it's important that he learns that actions have consequences, and I still think he should save up half the money for a new one. But, well, it's Christmas Day, isn't it? No harm in letting him have that one for the time being, is there?'

'But how did it get here?'

'She drove round with it. While you were spark out in bed.'

I threw my arms around him. 'Love, you are just wonderful,' I said. 'That's such a thoughtful thing to have done.'

'I was thinking about the rest of us as much as anything,' he said ruefully. 'He's bound to be on edge, you know. Thinking about tomorrow and seeing his mum and brothers and everything. Be good for all of us if he has something to take his mind off it, I thought.'

But as it turned out, Justin was anything but anxious on Boxing Day morning. Superficially, at least, he seemed really happy and excited. Perhaps I should have taken that in itself as an omen. Get over-excited about something in life and it's odds on that you'll be disappointed. And right now he was as bouncy as a rubber ball.

'Mum wasn't having her Christmas dinner yesterday,' he told me brightly, as we fed him an early breakfast of cereal, toast and orange juice. It was only just gone seven, and I was feeling the hour. We'd all really gone to bed much too late. 'She was saving it to have once I get there,' he went on. 'Bet my brothers were mad as hell about that!'

Despite my being pleased to see him animated – he'd become more withdrawn and uncommunicative as Christmas Day had worn on, which I'd put down to the twin evils of anti-climax after the presents and anxiety about seeing his mum – I offered up a silent prayer that fate would be on his side and that he *wouldn't* be disappointed. But the little I did know of his mother hardly filled me with optimism. He'd been in care since he was five. That spoke volumes in itself, let alone the fact that it had been a voluntary care order – she hadn't fought to keep him. Had given him up willingly. And why only Justin in care? Why not the other two as well?

'My social worker says she's got loads and loads of stuff for me,' he went on. 'I bet I have an even better Christmas today, don't you, Casey? I bet I will.'

Justin had spoken with Harrison Green on the phone a couple of days back – a mandatory phone call made when a child is first fostered just to check the child is okay and that things are going well. It's done in private, so the child can be honest if they're not happy. I hoped that wasn't the case with Justin, but who knew?

I told him that, yes, he most probably would have a wonderful second Christmas Day, while at the same time cursing Harrison for passing on such unnecessary details and over-exciting him. Why do that? Why get his hopes up about things he didn't actually know to be true? Especially when the history with Janice – that was his mother's name, apparently – had clearly shown they might well be dashed.

I waved them off, finally – it would be a long, boring six-hour drive there and back for Mike, bless him – and decided I should put it all out of my mind. Maybe his mother wasn't as bad as we suspected. And there was no getting away from it: I needed a break. Had it really only been a week since Justin had moved in with us – less than two since we'd all first clapped eyes on him? In some ways it felt like a lifetime. He'd certainly turned all our lives upside down. But I knew it would be easier once the new school term started. That was when we'd settle into some sort of routine. In the meantime, I'd better shower and dress and get going, I realised. Me and Kieron were going to spend the day round at Riley and David's. Mike would come there when he was back after dropping off Justin, and take me home a bit later for the blissful evening of relaxation we'd planned, just the two of us, in front of the TV. I couldn't have looked forward to anything more keenly, I decided, as I happily skipped back upstairs to get ready.

'Chinese or Indian?' Mike wanted to know. 'They're both open. I'm feeling curry, myself – you?'

'Don't care,' I called back to him as I plumped the sofa cushions, so we could sit down and watch yet another movie.

It was coming up to seven now, and the two of us were downing tools for the evening. Mike had returned around 2.30 and come straight round to Riley's, and we'd spent an enjoyable couple of hours there, just chatting about nothing; something which, like tonight, felt like a very distant luxury; one which I aimed to enjoy to the full.

Kieron was now out – some sort of lads' night on the tiles with a group of his college friends, and wouldn't be back again tonight. He was loving college and we were so happy to see him fitting in so well there. He was really interested in becoming a professional DJ on the club circuits, so had decided to enrol on a media studies course.

He was into his second term now and his tutor had said that he was making great progress. He'd also settled in socially and had made some solid friendships – he'd be sleeping over with one of his mates tonight, probably so we wouldn't see what sort of state he'd be in.

Mike filled me in on his first impressions of Justin's mother when we got home. Justin himself had apparently continued to be excited for the whole journey, babbling on about his little brothers and reminiscing about other Christmases and how exciting they had been. But when Mike asked anything specific, he tended to skirt around it; it was as if, Mike felt, he had this idealised perfect Christmas tableau in his mind, and that anything that reminded him of the reality had to be ignored, or the picture would be ruined.

Janice, Mike also told me, to my surprise, looked a bit like me. She was only a couple of inches taller than me and had the same dark eyes and black hair. He said she seemed very friendly and had invited him in. He'd felt reluctant but Justin was apparently insistent that he go in and meet his little brothers.

'Oh, I wish I'd been there with you,' I told him. 'I'd have loved to have met the little ones. What were they like? Did they look anything like Justin?'

Mike looked at me with that characteristically blank male expression. 'I suppose so,' he said. 'I didn't really notice.'

Typical male, I thought. Completely failed to get the facts. I shook my head. 'So what did the house look like, anyway? Were the kids well dressed? Were there books around? What sort of toys?'

'Hang on,' he said, pretending to rummage in his pocket. 'I think I have the full list right here. Complete with photographs …'

But I did wheedle some facts out of him eventually.

The family lived in a council house in the middle of a run-down estate, and the garden, Mike said, was full of rubbish. An old sofa, a load of broken kids' toys, and so on, were strewn around, while inside it was old fashioned, with an old fabric suite, seventies-style brown curtains and an ashtray that was overflowing with cigarette ends. The one incongruous thing was an enormous flat-screen telly and home-entertainment system, which apparently took up almost one whole wall of the living room.

He was satisfied, however, that Janice's welcome was authentic, and that she and Justin were genuinely pleased to see each other.

Mike looked tired now, and he'd have another early start tomorrow, as he was due to collect Justin from his mum's at around noon. So, satisfied that all was okay, I could finally relax – I intended to make the most of some 'us' time before then.

'*It's a Wonderful Life*' is on – perfect!' I said as he returned with the take-away menus. 'And it's only just started, too. Come on, snuggle up. You can put the order in when they have the next bunch of adverts.' I had held off from eating for most of the day, and was definitely looking forward to my Indian-style butter chicken and pilau rice, but I could hold off for another twenty minutes.

But whatever was going on in Jimmy Stewart's life, someone up there definitely didn't seem to like us. From the hall we could suddenly hear ringing – it was the phone. 'Who on earth could that be?' I said, as we both went to get up from the sofa at the same moment. 'Don't worry, love,' I told Mike, nudging him back down again. 'Stay put there. I'll go and see.'

I walked out into the hallway and picked up the receiver, by now half-expecting to hear either my mum or dad's voice – the rest of the family, like us, all used their mobiles these days. But before I could so much as get half a word out, I was greeted by the sound of an angry woman's voice.

'Can you come and get this little bastard?' she snarled at me. 'I fucking mean it. Come and get him *now*!'

I was absolutely gobsmacked and at first had no idea what was happening. 'I beg your pardon,' I said. 'Who is this?'

'It's me!' the woman snapped. 'Janice. Is that Casey?'

This was the first time I'd ever spoken to Justin's mother and I was mortified. 'Janice!' I said. 'What's the matter? What's wrong?'

I could hear her shouting, then, away from the phone, to someone else. 'You go near those kids, I'll kill you, you evil little bastard! You there, Casey?' She was back shouting at me again now. 'Can you here what's going on here? Can you?'

'Please Janice,' I said, trying to keep my own voice calm and level. Mike had appeared in the hall now and was looking at me quizzically. 'Just tell me what's going on there. Is Justin alright?'

She laughed sarcastically, but I could tell she was finding none of this any funnier than I was. 'Justin? Is fucking *Justin* alright? No he's not! He's not fucking right in the head!' She burst into tears then and now I could hear Justin in the background. He was shouting now: 'Casey! You'd better come and get me, Casey! I'm going to kill this fucking bitch in a minute!'

I tried hard to keep composed in the face of the reality that Mike would have to get him, and right away. 'Right, Janice,' I told her. 'Janice? *Listen*. Mike's going to set off now, okay. Just try to calm down … he'll get to you as soon as he can … tell you what, can you put Justin on the phone for me?'

I cupped my hand over the mouthpiece. 'I'm so sorry, love,' I mouthed at Mike, making faces to let him know that there'd been some sort of crisis. 'But you're going to have to go back and get him. Sounds like all hell's broken out up there. She's hysterical and crying and he's threatening to kill her. *God* … Can you just get ready while I try to calm things down?'

Mike, now resigned to the fact that our 'peaceful' night was not to be after all, left me trying to get to the bottom of things while he went to get himself ready for another long drive. In the meantime, I heard the phone being picked up again. 'Justin? Is that you, love? What's been happening? What's going on?'

He was crying too. Big snuffling sobs were pouring out of him in waves. 'Just get me, please, Casey. I'm going to kill the slag, I swear it!'

'Justin, love, it's okay. It'll all be okay. Mike's already left …' which was only half a lie since he was doing so even as I said it, bless him '– and he'll get there as soon as he can, okay?'

I could still hear Janice, close by. 'Little bastard!' she was shouting, and I presumed it was for my benefit. 'I've a good mind to call the fucking cops! Hit your fucking mother would you, you little bastard?'

'Casey,' Justin said then. 'I've gotta go now. Okay? I'll tell you later.' God, I thought miserably. Tell me *what*? 'Just tell Mike to hurry up, okay?'

And with that, he hung up. All we could now hear was the twang of James Stewart coming from the TV.

Yup, I thought grimly. Such a wonderful life.

It was in the small hours before Mike returned home with Justin. A very tense time since, in his rush to go and get him, Mike had not only left his mobile behind, he'd also left his wallet, and had been really concerned that he'd run out of petrol on the way home.

Justin looked shattered and in terrible pain and immediately went up to his bedroom. I wanted to reach out to him – if only just to hug him – but he seemed shut down and I sensibly didn't try to stop him. There was nothing to be achieved at this hour of the night. Let him sleep. That was the best thing. Time enough to deal with the whole sorry debacle in the morning.

Still, I felt desperately sorry for him; I was physically aching with the kind of pain any mother feels when one of her children is hurt or so deeply upset. Mike, too, looked tired – as he had every right to. I flicked the switch on the kettle and waited for him to speak.

'It was a bloody mess,' he said, once he'd sat down and got his freezing hands around a hot mug of coffee. 'She was already out and down the front path in her dressing gown before I'd so much as killed the engine and climbed out of the car. She was dragging the little ones with her, too. Couldn't shut her up – went off like a rocket – all about how she'd thought she'd surprise him by telling him she was pregnant – can you credit it? – and how he'd immediately lunged at her – by all accounts – and called her "fucking slut" and a "dirty whore".'

I shook my head, listening to all this. '*Pregnant?*'

'So she said. Anyway, she told me she hit him back when he said that, and he apparently hit *her* right back again, threatening to punch her in the stomach.'

I couldn't take it in, even though it was perhaps exactly what we should have expected, given the history. 'Oh, God,' I said, with feeling. 'What a mess.'

'Oh, but there's worse. He then "purposefully" – though how you can do that I don't know – threw up all over his unopened Christmas presents and then told her she could stick them all up her arse. The little ones were apparently crying and begging him to be nice to her, but his response, or so she tells me, was to start on them too – telling them that their mother was a slut and both their dads were junkies. And so on and so forth till we got the call.'

'Where was Justin while she was telling you all this? Did he have his own version?'

'No. Not with us. He was already by the car. He had run out ahead of her when I first pulled up. He was just sat in the road, against the wheel, on the far side, crying his bloody eyes out.' He shook his head. 'I can't believe it, Case. Really, I can't. How could the woman be so bloody insensitive that she had no idea – and she didn't, you could see that pretty clearly – how much she'd hurt him by what she'd said to him. Tell you what, I could have happily smacked her myself.'

'So did Justin tell you much when you set off?'

Mike shook his head. 'He was wretched, Case, really wretched. He said the first thing she told him was that they'd already done Christmas the day before, and that the second was that she had a surprise for him. And, I mean, if you say that to a kid ...'. He shook his head again, and I could see the whole thing had really got to him. 'But the surprise, of course, was that she was going to have a little girl. He said she really seemed to think the idea was funny – I think it's bloody *criminal* – and that she told him this girl of hers was going to be a princess and be spoiled and have everything. And be special. Not a "lunatic like him", those were his exact words'. He sipped his coffee and sighed as he set the mug down. 'And then he slept. All the rest of the way home.'

* * *

We went to bed heavy of heart, around three. How could any mother in the world say such wicked things to her own child? One thing was sure: if we had even the smallest chance of helping Justin, there was so, so much more that we needed to know.

Chapter 5

One of the main things Mike and I had to do as foster carers was to keep a log of anything and everything that happened during each placement: a comprehensive record of progress and pertinent information that could be placed on record in a child's file. In Justin's case, his file being something of a black hole up to now, I felt it was doubly important that I get everything down while it was fresh in our minds. I was also anxious to press John Fulshaw for more facts about Justin's mum and what exactly had been happening between them these past years. *Twenty failed placements*. I kept returning to that stark fact. If we wanted to help him we needed answers to so much. What had happened with this child? What had gone so badly wrong in so many placements? And we needed to know not just what had happened to him but *why*.

One thing was crystal clear. That Justin was struggling to hold it together. He was hurting a lot and, from what

Mike had witnessed at his mother's house, with very good reason. And there was something else, too. Since returning from there, he seemed to have decided, consciously or unconsciously, that he needed to take what his mum did out on me. Me and all women, perhaps.

Since Mike had pointed out the similarities between Janice and myself, I started to wonder if Justin sometimes found it difficult to separate his mother and me. It wasn't too far fetched an idea, I thought, not with all the trauma he had suffered in his short life.

'What you doing the cooking for?' he asked Mike, when he was in the kitchen preparing lunch the next day. 'You don't have a dog and bark yourself.' Surprised by that sort of comment coming from a child of eleven, Mike explained that not only didn't we talk like that in our house, we didn't believe it to be true, either. There was no hierarchy in our house, he explained. No order of importance. We were equals and in all things we worked as a team. If a meal needed preparing, then someone would prepare it. There was no law that said that someone had to be me. But Justin was adamant. 'That's women's work,' he said. And though Mike then explained that there was no such thing as 'women's work', he wouldn't have it. 'You won't ever catch me doing women's work,' he said firmly.

Later that day, he came down from where he'd been playing on his computer in his bedroom to find me, Riley, David and Kieron playing Scrabble.

'D'you want to join us?' Riley asked him. Justin looked shocked that she'd even spoken to him. 'Now, why would I want to do that?' he said. He then, very pointedly, turned to Kieron and David. 'Do you two want to play footie outside?' he asked them. 'We could set my new net up if you like.'

Riley set her Scrabble tiles down, her face fixed in a grimace. 'I was only trying to be friendly!' she snapped at him. 'And you can see perfectly well that they can't play "footie". We're in the middle of a game, if you hadn't noticed, so –'

'It's okay, Riley,' I interrupted, conscious of the sudden tension. 'I'm sure Justin didn't mean to be rude. How about you stay and watch who wins this round, eh, Justin? Then maybe the boys will have a kick about with you after.'

'Yeah,' added David, grinning. 'Stay and watch us anni-hilate these girls, yeah? Then we'll play footie.'

I loved David. He was such a great partner to Riley. Cheerful and funny, and also a rarity: a match for our very strong-willed daughter. Mike and I had both known him for longer than she had, as he was the son of a good friend of ours. I still didn't think Riley realised quite how big a hand her mum and dad had had in having them 'bump into' each other so often.

But like many men, he didn't see the signals the way us girls did, and got a scowl from his girlfriend for his well-meaning comment, made, I didn't doubt, to try and lighten up the situation. Justin sniggered, too, which annoyed Riley further. 'You don't think much of women, do you, Justin?' she observed sharply.

'*You don't think much of women, do you, Justin?*' he parroted. 'Nag nag bloody nag.' Upon which he turned on his heel and left the room.

The boys still seemed largely oblivious to what was going on here, but Riley and I weren't. Quite the opposite. We were seeing a pattern. And also a symptom, I thought – of a child trying hard to provoke a reaction.

'I definitely think he's trying to make you pay for what his mum said to him,' Mike suggested, confirming my own thoughts, when we had a few moments alone together later.

'Me *and* Riley,' I said, nodding. 'It's that whole black-haired woman thing, I'm guessing.' I sighed. 'I wish he'd actually sit down and talk to me, instead.'

But that wasn't happening. And there was more to come, too. It was obvious that we were really only scratching the surface of how much pain Justin was really suffering. The following morning I came down to find him sitting at the table, his empty breakfast dishes beside him, reading a magazine.

'You're up early, love,' I said. 'Mike make you breakfast, then, did he?'

He shook his head. 'Nah. He went to work ages ago. I made it myself.'

He seemed proud of having down that. Good, I thought. *Good.* That would give him some much needed points for his chart. And so much for his ideas about women's work …

I ruffled his mop of blond curls and he seemed happy to let me do so. 'What you reading?' I asked him.

'The magazine out of Mike's paper,' he said brightly. 'The one with all the telly stuff in it.'

As he would be, I guessed. He was mad about TV – the soaps, in particular. He was always flicking through the TV mags, or checking on the internet to see what his favourite characters were getting up to. He liked to know in advance what was going to happen and, if he was feeling particularly mischievous, he would often try to spoil the plot if an episode ended on a cliff-hanger, by telling us what would happen next.

I made myself a coffee and went upstairs to get showered, conscious of the positive mood I could sense. Perhaps today would see some positive developments between us, too. Perhaps he'd finally feel able to talk through what had happened. Cry, even. Let it all come out.

When I came back down though, he wasn't there any more – he'd gone into the living room to watch the telly. I picked up his plate and mug and got the cloth to wipe the kitchen table. It was then, as I picked up the magazine to wipe beneath it, that I noticed two holes in the page it was open at. Looking more closely, I realised that the holes weren't random, either – they'd been punched out through the eyes of a female celebrity.

I sat down, then, and went through the rest of the magazine, to find that exactly the same had been done on lots of pages; indeed, every dark-haired female celeb in the magazine had had her eyes carefully and precisely removed. I shuddered. It was creepy. It was also a worry. I must call John and tell him about this. It must be, I felt certain, part of a bigger picture, and would need adding to my log right away.

And that evening saw yet more disturbing behaviour. After cleaning away our dinner plates and checking tomorrow's menu, so that I could answer Justin's inevitable question about it, I flicked off the kitchen light and prepared to relax in the living room for the evening, beginning with watching *EastEnders*, as we habitually did.

It was only a short way into the programme, when Mike and I became aware that Justin was muttering to himself. He was sitting opposite the pair of us, on the other sofa, on his own, and seemed completely unaware that he was speaking out loud.

'Fucking slag,' he was muttering. 'Fucking dirty whore. You're gonna get what's coming. *Die*, you fucking bitch!'

We stared in shock at this, though he didn't even see us doing so. He seemed to be doing it to every female dark-haired character he saw. And as the main storyline at that time featured the black-haired Slater sisters, there were lots of dark-haired women on the screen throughout the show. He really didn't seem to know that he was doing it, either. It was if he was in some sort of trance.

Mike and I continued to watch him, both of us completely baffled, as he carried on throughout the whole episode. I was positive by now that he was unaware of his actions, and I wondered too, how this was going to pan out.

It was confirmed when it ended and the credits started rolling. The now familiar dark-eyed and menacing-looking grimace disappeared, almost in an instant. It was as if he mentally shook himself out of a trance, and came back into the room. He turned to me and grinned. 'I love *EastEnders*!' he said cheerfully. We could only nod and smile as he trotted out.

'What the hell?' Mike asked when he was sure the coast was clear.

'Love,' I said, shaking my head in disbelief, 'I can't even *begin* to give you a logical answer.'

'How many points has Justin got at the moment?' Riley asked me. She was on the phone a few days later, with a plan. 'It's David's last day off,' she explained. 'So we thought we'd go to the pictures. See a matinee. And we thought Justin might like to come along too.'

Bless her; I loved how she was so supportive of what we were doing. Especially since Justin often made it so hard for her to like him. I felt so proud of her. And David, as well.

'Great!' I said, mentally cheering at the prospect of a couple of hours to myself as much as anything. I had a call to make that needed Justin not to be around. 'It's also his last day before school starts, so your timing is absolutely perfect,' I told her. 'And, yes, I'm sure he has enough points on his chart to do something like that.' He had, too. Despite my continuing – and growing – concerns about his emotional state since the home visit, he was doing well in all practical respects. He was helping in the kitchen, fretting less volubly about mealtimes, helping tidy the garden, showering without having to be nagged and, I was pleased to note, even getting out a few of the things he'd so point-edly stashed away in his room. A trip out with Riley and David would be just the thing for him. 'He'll be thrilled,' I told her. 'I'll go and tell him the good news right away.'

Justin wasn't in his room when I went up to tell him, however, and I then realised I could hear the sound of the shower going. What *was* in residence, however, was a very strange smell. A sort of mixture of body odour and wet dog. And as soon as I smelt it, I was reminded that Kieron had already mentioned this to me. Kieron had said, just a couple of days ago, actually, that Justin's room smelt a bit like a hamster cage. At the time I hadn't given it much thought, but now I knew exactly what he meant. I wrinkled my nose as I poked my head in a bit further.

One of Justin's rules – and one of the ways he earned points – was that he was responsible for keeping his own room tidy. Not such a big deal, since he still had so little in it. I only went in there myself to collect things like empty mugs and laundry, and since he'd arrived with us, had only spent any time in there to strip and change his bedding for him. Even so, I decided, as I went to call to him in the bathroom, I'd say he'd been with us for coming up to four weeks, so his room could probably do with a bit of dusting and polishing – not to mention de-fumigating now, appar-ently. So once they'd gone out I decided I'd go in and give it a proper once-over, with the help of some elbow grease and bleach.

But that could wait till after I'd spoken to John, which I did straight after Riley and David had come to pick Justin up. There was such a lot to tell him that I spent a good ten minutes updating him on the events of the previous few days. 'I need information,' I told him, once I'd filled him in on what had happened between Justin and his mum. 'Surely you can find some files on him *somewhere*. His behaviour is really giving us cause for concern, and, now we've seen how bad things are with his mother, we know there's so much we aren't privy to. There must be. He has huge emotional issues.' I filled John in on the hole-punching business. 'And my instinct is that they are pretty long-standing. But what's the root of it all? What specifically? We feel we're stumbling around completely in the dark here, John. We can't help him without knowing properly about his background.'

I knew I must have sounded desperate, but the truth of it was that we were. If others didn't help us, by giving us some solid information on which to base how we dealt with him, then we couldn't really help Justin, could we? Only contain his behaviour, which, unless the underlying reasons for that behaviour were established and dealt with, was a pretty pointless thing to be doing. In my opinion we wouldn't have been doing our job properly, if these crucial questions continued to remain unanswered.

The good news, however, was that John hadn't been idle. Indeed, he'd been one step ahead of us already and had tracked down two of Justin's former social workers.

'One's retired,' he said, 'and one's now at a different authority. But both have agreed to meet me and discuss more of his background. I *am* on the case, Casey,' – he

68

laughed as he said this – 'I really am. I'll be back to you as soon as I can, promise.'

Feeling cheered by John's news I then trotted upstairs, armed with my collection of germ-busting sprays. There was no smell, however odd, that I, cleaner *extraordinaire*, couldn't get to the bottom of and completely expunge, and this one would be no exception.

My investigations bore fruit pretty quickly. The smell seemed to be coming from the big built-in cupboard in the corner; when I opened it, the stench increased tenfold. I began rootling around among the various shelves and boxes, and eventually came upon a supermarket carrier bag, full of something soft and squashy, and tightly tied at the top. When I finally managed to wrestle it open, my suspicions were confirmed. The stench was so strong, it literally exploded in my face. Gagging now, I peered in and looked at the contents: around ten pairs of dirty, smelly socks. But these were dirty, smelly socks way beyond any usual definition of such articles – and I thought that as someone who's been a mum to a teenage boy and no stranger to nasty, noxious niffs. They were stiff, too, so had obviously been there a while; they almost crackled as I pulled them from the carrier.

It was then when I saw something that immediately swept away all my previously light-hearted thoughts about boys and their attention to personal hygiene. No, these socks weren't just dirty, they were, all of them, bloody. The toe parts of all of them were liberally covered in the stuff, dried on and almost black in colour.

I got up from the floor and sat down on the bed, trying to make sense of what I was seeing. It was clear now just what the source of the foul smell was, clearer also why he'd so carefully squirrelled them away. Presumably till he could find some secret moment at some point, when he could wash them himself, away from my eyes.

I put the bag down, and started to search the room further. Which wasn't something I'd ever dream of doing with my own kids. Not something I'd do, period, in normal circumstances, with anyone. But this was serious. This was necessary, because some instinct drove me on. I didn't know what I was looking for, but I knew there would be something hidden somewhere. I just knew there was something else to find.

I was on autopilot now and went methodically through his room, inch by inch, searching carefully in every nook and cranny. And after the best part of an hour spent pretty much ransacking Justin's bedroom, I finally made my first find. I'd lifted up the mattress by now, to get a better look at the bed base, when I noticed a tiny tear in the mattress itself. It was very small, but also straight and clean and precise – it was clear it hadn't happened accidently. Very gingerly, I pushed a finger inside.

My fingertip found it – somewhat suddenly and painfully. I had caught it on the end of something sharp. Not wishing to slice off the top of my finger, I very carefully winkled it out. It was the blade from a craft knife. One that had come out of the set we had bought for him, I imagined.

The Boy No One Loved

Once again, instinct kicked in and drove me on. Brushing aside my initial feelings of dread at what I might find next, I began my second search with renewed vigour. My attention to detail wasn't disappointed. Within half an hour I had a decidedly grim haul, all laid out on the bedroom floor around me: a variety of knives and blades of all kinds, with which he'd obviously been cutting himself. There were some scissors, which I recognised, that I thought I'd mislaid – I'd even enlisted Justin's help in trying to find them, I remembered – and two or three disposable razor blades, with the plastic blade holders melted off, which meant he must also have found a lighter or matches. Plus there was a small vegetable knife, which I hadn't ever seen before, and a Stanley knife, which I guessed he might have taken from our tool box.

It was a gruesome display, and I sat there and surveyed it with both horror and a great sense of sadness. What would drive any boy to do such a thing?

This couldn't have been new. Someone, *surely*, must have known this. *This* was how much Justin was hurting.

Chapter 6

'I just can't help it,' Justin said. 'I know I shouldn't do it, but I can't help it.'

It was the following morning, and Justin and I were sitting in his bedroom, where, after much soul searching, I'd finally confronted him.

'I know, sweetheart, I know,' I said. 'But we can't have you hurting yourself like this, can we? It must really hurt you, and not only that, if I don't know about it, I can't help you to keep those cuts clean. They might have got infected, and could have turned really nasty, and then where would we be, my love, eh?'

I'd been feeling wretched since I'd made my grim discovery. I'd lain awake and tossed and turned all night, berating myself that I'd not been aware of his self-harming before. Surely, or so my mind went, with my long experience of damaged children, I should have noticed *something* that would have given him away? How had alarm bells not rung when I'd lost the scissors, for example?

I'd told Mike about how I'd even had Justin helping me to look for them, and how angry I was at myself that it hadn't occurred to me then. And how had I completely failed to see anything? Notice his feet? Now I'd found what I had, it was clear that they must have been in shreds. And this child wasn't just a visitor – he *lived* with us. I felt so guilty and angry at myself. How did he manage to keep something like that hidden from us so well?

'Because he's a very private person, Case,' Mike had pointed out to me. 'You *know* that. Keeps himself to himself. When exactly do you think you might have seen something? He's either fully dressed, or in pyjamas, and he's never without his slippers –'

'And now we know why!'

'Come on, Case. Don't be so hard on yourself. It's not as if he's a tot that you'd have to help to wash and dress, is it?'

Mike had been right, of course, but I still felt this huge sense of guilt. From now on I must be so much more vigilant. I looked at Justin's anguished face now, and wondered if I should put my arms around him. It was difficult to judge whether to risk it or not. I didn't want him to clam up now he looked like he was talking to me at last, and the physical contact might just make him do that.

He was in his pyjamas now – and the ubiquitous slippers – lying on his bed, watching cartoons. Or at least he had been, before I'd come in to confront him with my findings.

'Come on, love. Let me take a look at those feet of yours,' I coaxed instead. 'Let me get them cleaned up for you, at least.'

I kept my expression neutral as Justin slowly pulled off his slippers, though it was as hard a thing to do as I'd had to in a long time. His feet were, as I'd expected, in a terrible mess. You could see this was something he'd been doing for a long time. The nail beds looked infected and the skin around them looked horrible. He obviously dug into them regularly, causing copious bleeding. There were scabs and livid patches all over them. It pained me to think about how much this must have hurt, and again I mentally kicked myself for not realising.

I could have gone to the bathroom at that point, gathered some supplies and got the job done, but something told me that if I did so I might miss my moment. I got a very strong feeling that he wanted to talk. Just didn't know how to start. He was staring at his feet now, as if seeing them with new eyes.

'You know what I think, love?' I said, sitting down beside him on the bed. 'I think you must have been hurting a very great deal on the inside to want to hurt yourself so much on the outside.' I paused for a moment to let this sink in, then continued. 'I also know you've had a lot of bad stuff happen in your life. When you were little?' He nodded. 'And something else I know is that when young kids go through bad stuff – when kids are too young to really understand what's happened to them and why, well, sometimes it makes them really angry when they're older, and

74

then they do things like you've been doing to your feet. It's not your fault, Justin. I'm not cross with you. You do understand that, don't you?'

He was silent for a long, long moment, head hanging, then he lifted it and turned to me, his eyes meeting mine. And suddenly came this whole rush of words. 'What's to understand, Casey? My life's been fucking shit! She's a bitch, that's all. A bitch. She got rid of me, told me all this stuff about how I was trouble and everything. But she kept Alfie and Mikey, didn't she? *Didn't* she? I understand alright. I understand all of it.' He was crying now, I could see, except so softly and so silently. Leaking tears, almost. It wasn't anger. It was if he had no fight left in him. Now instinct told me that it would be okay to touch him, so I moved closer and put my arm around his shoulders. I waited for him to stiffen, but he didn't. Quite the contrary. He leaned into me, burying his head into my chest, and now he started sobbing much harder.

'It was shit,' he said again. 'Shit. I mean, I knew she was on drugs. Couldn't not know. All the kids used to take the piss all the time. But I never knew it was heroin. I never knew that. I mean I knew the name of it, and everything, but not what heroin was, what it *does*. All I knew was that she never got any food for us. Never fed us. An' Alfie only needed fucking baby milk, that's *all*. An' she never got it …'

I squeezed his shoulder. 'I can't imagine how hard it must have been to live like that.'

He lifted his head away a little to look at me again. 'Casey, can I tell you something?'

'Course you can, love,' I answered. 'Though there's something I need to tell you first, okay?'

I hated having to do it, but I really needed to say it. It was an essential, integral part of my job that I say it. 'It's just that you have to know, Justin, that if it's something really, really bad that you're going to tell me, that I have to share it. You understand? So that we can *all* try to help you. Okay?'

He nodded, though I wasn't completely sure it went in. He seemed more focussed on continuing now than listening. And I needed to let him.

'It was Alfie and Mikey,' he went on. 'And we were, like, starving. All of us were. I couldn't even remember the last time we'd got some food, because she'd been flat out, just, you know, lying there mostly, for days. And now she was out and I was minding them and she didn't come back, and they just kept shouting and crying from upstairs and I didn't know what to do. But then I remembered in next door's garden they had stuff growing. Lots of things. An' they had rhubarb. You know rhubarb?'

I nodded. 'Yes. I know rhubarb.'

'So I climbed on the dustbins and over the fence and I stole a load of sticks of it, just so they had something. But when I took it up to them, they were in their cot together, and they were just sitting there in it, nappies off, eating their own shit. Eating it, Casey! Both of them. Sitting there, eating their own shit!'

'Oh, love, that's horrible …'

'She didn't care, though!' He was having to gulp back the tears now. 'She didn't even *care*! And she'd, like, come back, and bring all her druggy mates with her, and they'd just be there, then, downstairs. All laid out on the sofas and on the floor. And the babies would be crying, and no-one would even *hear* them!'

I could sense the anger building in him as he recounted all this to me. I was trying to picture the horror of it, and I was beginning to feel physically sick. I could sense, though, that I needed to brace myself even further, because it seemed clear to me that this was just the start of it.

I didn't want him to become angry; not so angry that he became physical and unable to control his emotions. I just wanted him to keep talking to me. Getting it all out. Because I felt that this might be a major breakthrough. No, I *knew* this was a major breakthrough, him sharing all this with me. And there *was* more to come. He rubbed his sleeve across his face, and continued, his body still leant into me, the side of his head a warm weight against my upper arm. I held him tighter. How many times in his life had this child been cuddled, I wondered. Could you maybe count the times on the fingers of one hand? And what must that do to a child?

'She had this party, Casey, one time,' he continued. 'A whole bunch of people. Late at night. We were all of us supposed to be upstairs sleeping, but we couldn't. It was mad down there. Mad. Loads of music. Lots of shouting. They kept playing this record. You know? Like, over and over and over. UB40 it was. You know them? My mum liked them a lot.

'Then this man came upstairs. Just appeared in the bedroom doorway. And he, like, gave me this pound coin and asked me if I wanted to come down. You know. "Join the party" was what he actually said to me. An' I was excited when he did that. I got a whole pound. There might be more. There might even be some *food* down there. So I went down with him and there were about, I guess, six or seven people in there. Mostly men. One other woman. I didn't know who she was. Never seen her before. And then this bloke said did I fancy playing a game of dares with him. An' I didn't know what he was on about, and he said it was just this game ...'

He was stumbling over his words now, as if he couldn't find the right ones. How hard must it be to recount such grim memories? 'A game?' I asked.

Justin nodded. 'And then he undid his trousers. And then he got my hand and put it in there and made me grab, you know, inside there. And he was laughing. They all were laughing. Even my mum was laughing. And they said I had to keep it there until they'd counted up to sixty out loud.'

His face contorted as he said this, his words now punctuated by heavy sobs. I stroked his hair. 'I know,' I said softly. 'I know, Justin. I know ...'

We sat for some moments, then, without speaking further. But just as there's a lull in the eye of a storm, I suspected there might be more. And there was.

The house smelled like it normally did, on that chilly November morning. Smelled of that familiar mix of urine and cigarettes.

The Boy No One Loved

The heavy curtains were drawn completely across the dirty front-room windows and the sofa had been pushed back to make more room on the floor. And there, amid the sea of squashed beer cans, overflowing ashtrays, the filthy coffee table, all the sweet wrappers, lay Justin's mother, spark out and barely conscious, on the sheepskin rug in front of the electric fire.

'Suck it!' barked the man who had Justin's head clamped firmly between his hands. 'Suck it, you little bastard!' He pushed hard, frighteningly hard, against the little boy's head, squashing his terrified face into his groin.

Justin was gagging and wriggling, and desperately trying to catch sight of his mother. He couldn't understand why she wasn't helping him. Why was she letting this man do this to him?

'You better make him do it right,' the man was growling, 'you fucking bitch. Or you can kiss goodbye to your fucking gear, believe me.'

He punched Justin in the back, then, causing him to struggle even harder. And now, at last, his mother became animated. Rising unsteadily to her knees, she shuffled across the cord carpet to kneel down beside them. 'Come on, baby,' she whispered in his ear. 'Be good for Uncle Phil now. C'mon, babe. You know mummy needs her medicine.'

It wasn't the first time. He didn't think it would be the last time. But what could he do except what his mum was asking? So he squeezed his eyes tight shut and thought about Father Christmas – thought hard about what he might bring him if he was a good boy. And about how important it was that mummy got her medicine. And he wanted her to have it. He really, really wanted her to have it. If she had her medicine she'd soon be all happy again, and might even want a cuddle on the sofa. So he just got on with it, praying that it might soon be over, and concentrating really hard on not being sick – he knew that would make Uncle Phil really angry.

And then, suddenly it was done, and the man pushed him away, and he could scramble at last towards the arms of his mother, trying to wipe the salty liquid from his mouth as he did so. But she was out of the door already, gone to get some tin foil, he guessed, for the man to put her medicine into.

Justin didn't mind now. It was over and he could wait. In fact he waited very patiently, curled into the corner of the sofa, chilly in just his underpants. Because he knew, as he watched them hold the lighter flame underneath the tin foil, that soon – as soon as they'd sucked up all the smoke through her broken pens – she'd become different, and happy, and maybe his again.

Sure enough, she soon flopped down beside him, smiling dreamily. But there was no time for cuddles. She had other ideas.

'C'mon, babe,' she murmured at him. 'Be a good boy, babe. Go and get dressed now. It's time to go to school.'

He tried to argue – he wanted to stay and stroke her mass of bouncy black curls for a bit – but Uncle Phil roughly cupped his face in his big smelly hand and said, 'Do as you're told. It's school time!' So there was nothing else for it. He'd have to do as he was told.

His uniform was crumpled on the floor in the kitchen, exactly where he'd left it yesterday. And, just like yesterday, there was nothing there to eat. There was ketchup and there were Oxos and there was an inch or two of brown sauce, but nothing you could eat for breakfast. No proper food. He eventually found a single ginger biscuit, so he stuffed that in his mouth, and listened, as he dressed, to Uncle Phil shouting at Dylan, his mum's dog. His mum, he thought, would probably be asleep now anyway.

He tiptoed upstairs. His brothers were sleeping too. And if they were asleep they weren't going to ask for food or wail at him. Satisfied, he quietly left the house.

'Who you think you're talking to, you stinking little scruff?'

Justin turned to see two boys he knew, both headed towards him. He was in the park now, having taken the long route to school. It was much too early to go the road way so he thought he'd go through the park and skim some pebbles across the duck pond.

He dropped the stone he'd been holding and was about to throw, and shook his head. *'No-one,'* he answered. These were bad kids, he knew. Always getting into trouble with the police and causing trouble on the estate His mum said so. And he should keep well away.

'You're a fucking little oik,' said the bigger one. *'And your mum's a dirty whore.'*

'Shut up!' said Justin even though he knew he shouldn't dare to. *'Or she'll be round to your house and sort you out!'*

'What, give me dad a blow job?' the other boy taunted, pushing Justin. *'She's a fucking junkie, she'll do owt to get a score.'*

Justin couldn't help it. He burst into tears. *'Just leave me alone, I want to go home now,'* he cried, which made the two boys laugh at him even more. Then one of them, obviously still in the mood for more tormenting, pushed Justin over and quickly slipped off both his shoes. *'Without these?'* he taunted, before *lifting them high in the air and then lobbing them straight into the middle of the duck pond.*

'Hey!' said Justin, scrambling to his feet and brandishing his fists now. He threw himself at the older boy and started to pummel him, which only made both boys laugh even harder. But not done yet with humour, and before he could do anything to stop it happening, they grabbed his arms and legs, tipped him up and ducked his whole head into the water.

They then pulled him out, sniggering at all his coughing and his spluttering. 'Bye, freak,' they said. 'See you at school.'

It was some minutes before he found the energy to get up again, almost all of which he spent in silent contemplation of the sky. He was freezing, he was soaking, and he was covered in mud. He had no shoes, and he knew there was no way he'd be able to find them. They were too far out in the water. It was too dangerous. He might drown. He couldn't go to school now. He wouldn't go to school now. He'd go back home, he thought, and tell his mum what had happened. He'd limp home, in the freezing cold, barefoot. What else could he do?

But when he got home, his mother wasn't there.

Chapter 7

We'd been sitting there together for an hour by now. An hour in which I'd had to struggle to keep myself together as Justin talked. I knew it was essential that I do that, however. If I conveyed even a fraction of the rage and disgust I was feeling as he described the grim details of his early childhood to me – childhood, what bloody childhood? – I was sure he'd clam up and find it impossible to go on. These were dark secrets he was sharing and I knew from long experience that children who've been involved in such ordeals bore scars that, even with the best care and support in the world, would probably never really fully heal. Scars that ate away at their minds and hearts, like some horrible cancer, and muddied every aspect of their sense of themselves. Like any other child ever born, Justin would have felt guilty. Would have felt that in some way he deserved what had happened to him. Because that, tragically, was what children did.

I wiped the tears that were forming steady tracks down both of our cheeks now, wanting nothing more than to beat the living daylights out of all these monsters. I knew I needed to keep a professional head on at all times, and that, considered rationally, these 'monsters' were also probably just people who had been profoundly damaged themselves, but, at that moment, I didn't quite know how to feel anything for them but utter fury.

What I did know was that anything in my power I could do to help Justin, I would do. He deserved so much better than the hand life had dealt him. He deserved happiness. Deserved nothing less. No child did. But also because not only had the adults in his life let him down, big time, but their cruelty and neglect had also sealed his fate with all his peers; causing him to be a target for bullies.

But now Justin, still for the moment, and close beside me, once again brought me out of my reverie.

'That was the day,' he said.

'The day?'

'The day I burned the house down.'

The day I burned the house down. I took this fact in. Not 'the house burned down' but '*I* burned the house down'. This was just heartbreaking to hear.

But I knew better than to react to it. Instead I remained silent and let him continue.

'I got back there,' he went on, 'and my brothers were in such a state. She'd just left them! Just gone and left them! Can you believe she'd do that? And they were in such a right state. An' crying. And wanting food. And I just couldn't bear it. I had nothing to give them and I didn't know what to do. And just thought ...'

He trailed off. 'That you couldn't cope with things any more?'

I felt him nod against me. 'I just couldn't. Casey. I just couldn't. And the dog eating their shit, and all their crying, and everything ... I just couldn't believe she'd *do* that. Can you?'

It took Justin another hour to recount to me the full horror of the events of that day. That day that had been described to Mike and I so dispassionately, so matter of factly. The neatly recorded detail of this five-year-old child who'd been playing with matches and, as a result, had accidentally burned the house down and then been placed in care. This five-year-old who was such a handful that his poor mother simply couldn't handle him and had had no choice but to allow social services to take him. And who could blame her? After all, this was a child who, in all the reports written about him since then, was 'trouble', was 'off the rails', was a 'bully'.

Except, perhaps all those reports *weren't* true. Or wouldn't have been, had his early life been different. There was clearly so much more that went on that day – and the days before it; the whole lifetime before it – that social services didn't know anything about. I worked in the care sector. I had worked for several years in a big comprehensive with a very mixed intake, so I wasn't naive. Yet I simply couldn't comprehend that such things – such major things as a heroin-addict mother and the way she was failing her three tiny children – went undetected these days. Surely some neighbour or some friend of the family must have noticed? Surely anyone who had anything to do with the family, however briefly, must have known that things weren't right?

Listening to Justin now – hearing exactly what *did* happen, and how the fire had been deliberate, not the result of any playing with lighters or matches – it seemed clear to me that something had snapped in him that day, taken him past the end of his tether. And no wonder. He was five and had been living in hell, and not a single adult had done anything to help him. The sexual abuse, the crying babies, the bullying – it didn't matter which. What most mattered, from what Justin was saying to me now, was that in that instant of returning home, wet, cold, miserable and needing his mum, he just knew it would never get better, never change, and that this was one way to get something done. He couldn't have known what – he was far too young to make such rational decisions. Cliché or otherwise, it had been a cry for help.

Justin had no explanation, and I didn't press for one, for what made him do what he did. And how could he? He'd been five. Not this sad, damaged, self-harming eleven-year-old, that no-one had ever seemed to love, who was cradled in my arms now. But just *five*. Would he even have *had* an explanation? I doubted it. He just knew, seeing the dog licking the shit from his brother's cot bars, that this was it. This was life. And he simply couldn't cope with it any more.

'I wanted Dylan to die,' he told me, though I hadn't actually asked him about it; I had only wondered, as I assume other people had before me, why he'd got his little brothers out of the house but not the family pet. But then, clearly, this was no sort of 'family' pet.

'I hated him,' Justin said. 'I hated him because she loved him. He was *her* dog and she loved him better than us. She used to cuddle him and pet him. Do you know, she even had a photo of him on the front-room wall. Not of us kids. Oh no, just the dog. And he got food – she always seemed to be able to get food for *him*. An' I wanted to pay her back. Teach her a lesson. And I did.'

I felt a new tightness in my throat as I thought about just how high a price that five-year-old boy paid for exacting that revenge. 'I know, love,' I said soothingly. 'I know.'

It had taken some time for social services to track down Justin's mother on the day of the fire. She'd been with her 'boyfriend', somewhere else on the estate, far enough away not to hear either the commotion or the sirens. It had been the next-door neighbours who'd called the fire brigade to alert them about the house fire, and they'd arrived to find both Justin and his little brothers all huddled beneath the duvet, in the garden, the little ones terrified, but Justin himself seemingly mute.

'She didn't want them to take me,' he said, as I finally gathered my wits about me and began dealing with cleaning and dressing the cuts and gouges on his feet. He seemed so much calmer now he'd told me his story. 'She didn't want them to at all,' he repeated. 'She did love me an' my brothers really …' he paused here. 'She did. But she had to, they told her she did. They said if she didn't let them take me away she'd have to go to prison. So I had to go with them. Or else she'd have gone to prison.'

I bit my tongue, remembering John's words when he'd first told us about Justin. *Voluntary care order*. That much was crystal clear. 'I know, love,' I said again. 'It must have been horrible. Horrible for all of you. There,' I finished, beckoning him to inspect his cleaned wounds. 'It's important we keep them clean now, so they'll heal.' I looked closely at him, realising just how much time had passed now. We'd been up here for hours. 'You must be hungry,' I said. 'It's way past your normal breakfast time. Shall we go down and I'll get you something nice to eat?'

But he wasn't hungry – a first – and also, for the first time since his arrival, he wasn't bothered about the clock or the schedule either. He told me he just wanted to lie on his bed for a bit. Chill out and watch some cartoons.

'You sure?' I said, making to rise from the bed now. 'I could make you some toast and bring it up.'

Justin shook his head, and then did something that shocked me to the core. He spread his arms and leaned in towards me for a hug. 'I love you, Casey,' he said, as I encircled him in my arms. 'I do. I really love you, you know.'

Unable to speak now, for fear of breaking down completely, I simply nodded and hugged him tightly till he released me, then left the room.

By the time I was downstairs, my brain was whirring with it all. This was incredible progress. Progress, and also a real insight into more of Justin's past. I must speak to John Fulshaw as soon as I could, I realised, while everything was really clear in my mind. At last I really felt we could do something to help Justin. But I got no further – my emotions were just too overwhelming to be tucked into a pocket in my mind, labelled 'work'. So instead I just sat down and cried.

Chapter 8

It was the following Saturday morning and I was on pins.

I'd had long conversations with both John Fulshaw and Harrison Green, filling them in about what Justin had told me, and even though I understood completely that this was my fundamental responsibility as a foster carer (and one I would never consider running away from), I still felt terribly anxious about the consequences when I explained to Justin that both of them would now want to talk to him too. It had to be done, of course: quite apart from the importance of this to Justin's psychological progress, there were larger issues, too, not the least of which was the fact that Janice still had Justin's two brothers with her, and was expecting another. Was she still a user? Was she still fraternising with abusers, come to that? And, crucially, would these revelations involve further investigation of her by social services? If that happened, she would know where the revelations had come from, further jeopardising their already fractured relationship. That, above all, made me feel terrible about it. For I felt sure what her response to him would be.

So I felt bad. I had a powerful sense of just how big a thing it was for Justin – so private, so unable to get close to anyone, so mistrustful of the adult world – to open up to me, in many ways a stranger still myself, and to share his darkest, most painful memories. I had a strong hunch, despite my having pointed out that I'd have to share them, that he would see this as a major betrayal. And why wouldn't he? He was eleven; how could he properly understand such things?

And it would turn out that I was right to be so fearful.

I'd elected to forgo a Saturday shopping trip with Riley (reluctantly, as quality 'girly' time with my daughter was, and is, one of my favourite things of all) so that I could be sure of having a period of time when Justin and I would be alone in the house. Mike always gave Kieron a lift to play football on Saturdays, and would stay to cheer him on from the sidelines.

And now that time had come and I was as antsy as hell. 'Come on you two,' I nagged Kieron and Mike. All three of them were playing Football Manager on the Playstation – 'boys' together. As happy and relaxed a family scene as you could wish for. Justin had been in a good mood all morning, in fact, which made me feel more nervous still. 'You're going to be late for kick-off if you don't hurry up. And *that* game –' I pointed towards the TV and console – 'will still be here when the two of you get back.'

I was keen – we all were – that Justin get out and get more exercise, not only because he was carrying a few extra pounds, but also because we knew the emotional value of exercise; something which, for a stressed child with so many problems, such as Justin, could make a real difference to his mental state. And if he could find a sport or activity that he liked and had a flair for, it could provide a place in which he could channel his anger and aggression, and, who knew, if he worked at it, develop his self-esteem.

But despite much encouragement from both Mike and Kieron, we'd yet to persuade Justin of the pleasures of the great outdoors. Mike joked that he was afraid to even go and watch a game, just in case somebody accidentally kicked a ball in his direction. Maybe we would convince him eventually, but right now the PlayStation and TV held much more attraction, as it often did for children with difficult backgrounds and few friends. Today, though, he seemed happy, grabbing the controller from Kieron and grinning. 'Yeah, go on, you two,' he agreed. 'Leave this with me. I can make sure your teams lose so I go up the league.'

'Muuuummmmm!' Kieron whined at me. 'Don't let him do that! It took me ages to get up to that position!'

I pulled a face at him. 'Kieron, honestly. You are *how* old, exactly? C'mon Mike, love, take him away so he can play with the big boys!'

With more ribbing and a touch more teasing from Justin, they were finally out of the front door and the house was still. Justin went back to the PlayStation and I decided to leave him for a short while, mostly so I could gather my own thoughts before confronting the unpalatable task I had in store.

Fifteen minutes later, it being lunchtime, I decided to call him to the kitchen. I'd made us both sandwiches and put the plates on the table. He pulled out a chair, sat down and picked up his.

'I was only messing about, Casey,' he said to me, without prompting. 'I won't really mess up Kieron's game.'

I was touched at this. 'I never thought you would, love. And nor did Kieron. Just a bit of fun, eh? Do you want a glass of milk?'

He nodded, and remembered to swallow before replying. 'Yes, please,' he said. 'And can I have some crisps, too? I'm starving.'

'You're always starving!' I answered, going to the cupboard to get a packet. 'I'd think something was seriously up if you weren't!' I came to the table then, sensing my moment. 'By the way, love,' I said lightly. 'I've been meaning to tell you. You know the chat we had Thursday? You know, about your mum and stuff?'

Silence. He just sat and stared at the sandwich, which he had just put back down on his plate. Shit, I thought. *Shit*. I should have left this till later. Give him a couple of days to regain his equilibrium. But I'd started now, so I'd have to see it through. 'Well, the thing is,' I went on, 'you remember me telling you I'd have to speak to Harrison and John about some of it? Well, I've had a chat with them, because … well, because some of it's kind of worrying, isn't it, love?

And they need to understand about some of the things that have happened to you so that they can help you too. As well as me …' I stopped then. In fact, I was literally stopped in my tracks, because Justin was staring at me and his face had completely changed. Even though I knew that at any moment there'd be a huge eruption, I just couldn't help but be mesmerised by his expression. I'd never seen anything quite like it – before or since. It was honestly like looking at one of those horror films, in which a human morphed into a werewolf in slow motion. His eyebrows lowered and seemed to merge into one long angry line, while his eyes darkened – really darkened; almost to black. His cheek-bones became prominent and his mouth curled into a kind of sneer. I had to keep telling myself *he's just a child, he's just eleven, that's all* – because it really was that chilling to observe.

He slowly raised his head – *here it comes, I thought, here it comes* – placed both hands on the table, rose, and pushed his chair back.

'Don't worry, Justin,' I tried. 'They won't *tell* anyone. It's confidential. They won't do anything to get you into trouble. You're *not* in trouble. They just want to help you. We *all* do!'

'You fucking bitch,' he said quietly. In fact, his voice was astonishingly level. Even so, I knew this could very soon get ugly.

'Justin,' I said firmly. 'Please don't speak to me like that. You'll lose points now, and that's such a shame. You've done so well so far today.' I was clutching at straws and I knew it.

'Fuck the points,' he growled at me. 'And fuck you too. You said I could trust you!'

'But you *can*!'

'No I can't! You're a liar. A fucking liar! Why did you have to tell them? Why? I'm not staying here.' He kicked the chair out of his way. 'I'm not staying! You're just like my mother!'

He then grabbed his plate – *smash*. It hit the kitchen wall, hard, and I ducked out of the way simultaneously, instinctively, even though I could see that, thank God, he hadn't actually aimed it at me. That sort of aggression, I reflected, even in the midst of what was happening, might have proved a step way too far to get back from. But then, I'd yet to know what was still to come.

He started punching the table now, with clenched fists, making the rest of the things on it dance and clatter across the surface, like flotsam and jetsam on a stormy sea.

I snatched up my own plate, before it too was smashed into pieces. 'Justin!' I had raised my voice now. I had to stay calm but in charge. 'Go to your room until you're calm! I will not speak to you while you're reacting like this.' I picked up his milk glass, as well. 'I know you're angry,' I went on. 'I *understand* that. And I'm sorry you feel that way, I really am. But I will not have you speaking or behaving in this manner. Go on!' I finished, trying to inject my voice with maximum authority. 'Move it, okay. Move it *now*!'

Please, I thought, watching him decide whether to obey me. *Please*, I thought, *don't make this any worse. Just go.* But I could sense his indecision so I rammed my point home again. 'Justin, I am not going to talk to myself here! *Room*!' I jabbed a finger towards the door. 'Room, *now*!'

That did it. He stormed to his room, slamming every door he walked through, screaming obscenities as he went.

I touched my chest. My heart was pumping like a train. It was as if the whole fabric of the house was shuddering.

After I'd cleared up the broken crockery and re-established some sort of order, I sat in the kitchen for some time, feeling terrible. I had *had* to tell – it was my job to pass on things like this – but I felt I'd gone about things all wrong. Surely I could have prepared Justin more, or found a better way to tell him what had had to happen. It really brought it home to me how much I still had to learn about this new career I'd chosen – Mike and I had both chosen – not to mention having a very stark and physical reminder of what an incredibly big and demanding job it was.

I took a deep breath and stooped to collect a small piece of broken plate under the table, which I'd missed, surprised to see that I was physically shaking. In all my time in the school unit, I'd never felt quite so vulnerable and shaken up. How the hell had an eleven-year-old reduced me to this? I reached for my cigarettes on autopilot and went outside to light one. But I couldn't because my hands wouldn't stay still long enough to make the lighter work.

How could this be? I had worked with some of the most difficult children for years, and I tried hard to look back and think of a comparable event. I was angry with myself, and with the situation too. It seemed that the one time, in fact, the *first* time, that I had an 'in' to Justin, I'd had to – through no fault of my own – then destroy it. Yes, it was the protocol, but it was bloody hard to swallow, and I wasn't sure I trusted the protocol any more.

It took me a long time to calm down, and once I had, I tried to call Mike, but he obviously had no signal at the football ground because his phone was going straight to voicemail. I knew he wouldn't be back till teatime either, and I wasn't sure what to do. I thought about asking Riley to come over but I was worried that might just make Justin worse.

I spent some time feeling completely undecided, just standing in the conservatory, smoking, staring out into the garden. Should I go up to him and see if he'd calmed down, or should I not? In the end, I opted not to because I thought it might just exacerbate the situation and ignite a further confrontation. I was also nervous and wary about facing him again, alone. He'd scared me quite a bit and I had knots in my stomach just thinking about going up there. Best to just leave him and hope he stayed put and had calmed down by the time Mike got home.

In the meantime, I needed to get on with something, so after I'd cleared the last of the mess up and binned the remains of Justin's sandwich, I set about preparing that evening's tea. I'd planned home-made chicken korma with rice – one of Kieron's favourites, and now methodically pulled the ingredients from the fridge. Chicken breasts, peppers, onions and garlic, all of which I assembled and started chopping and crushing. It was strangely therapeutic, doing this rhythmic, mindless task and, minute by minute, I felt the tension in my shoulders begin to ease. I even began to wonder, as I steadily grew calmer, if perhaps I was over-reacting to what had just happened. After all, I had expected an outburst from him hadn't I? And maybe it was justified, too.

I'd been at it for about half an hour when Justin suddenly reappeared in the kitchen, startling me, as I hadn't heard him come down the stairs. He said nothing; just took up his place at the table once more. Taking his lead, I decided to say nothing either. I just smiled but he immediately turned his face away.

It seemed he was determined to get my attention, for all that, because he began tapping cutlery against the table top. Not for long though; he soon tired of that, and got up once again – coming over quite close beside me, at the worktop. Here he picked up the flat knife – the one I'd just used to crush the garlic cloves – and started running it up and down the worktop. He then put it down and went over to the cooker, where the frying pan of chicken was sizzling. Now he picked up the wooden spoon that was resting in the pan and began tapping it rhythmically against the side of it. The growing tension was once again almost palpable.

'Can you stop doing that please, Justin?' I asked him levelly. But he ignored me and simply carried on. I left it for a minute then asked him again. 'Justin, can you please stop that?' I repeated, this time more firmly. But once again he carried on regardless.

I was well aware something was building again, but was entirely unprepared for what happened next. Even before I could properly see what was happening, Justin suddenly lunged for my knife block, grabbed a knife out of it, then leapt up, in a single bound, onto the worktop.

Both astonished at his agility – so much for his apparent lack of athleticism – and also terrified, as he was now towering over me, I watched horrified as he brandished it, his face set in that scary rictus mask again, screaming obscenities at me and becoming more and more incoherent, as the words tumbled out – he hated me, he was going to stab me, I was a fucking crap mother. But when he yelled that I preferred the dog to him, it really brought me up short – we didn't own one – and I realised he was talking as if he was confusing me with his mother. I wasn't even sure he was fully *compos mentis* at that moment, and I knew I had to think fast, and on my feet.

'Put the knife down,' I said firmly. 'Justin, just put the knife down.' But he was almost blue in the face now, and I could see he wasn't hearing me. He had completely zoned out and gone to that other place. It was then, in a flash, that I had an idea. One that definitely wasn't by the book. Not any foster-carer's handbook I'd ever seen, anyway.

Having considered two things – that Justin had picked up the smallest knife in the block, and also his great love of films, and one film in particular – I lunged myself for the biggest one, which I whipped from its slot and brandished every bit as menacingly as he had.

Then, in my very best Australian accent, I said, 'Call that a knife? That's not a knife. *This* is a knife!' And then paused, my breath held waiting for his response.

He just stared, now stock still, looking incredulously at me, then, to my mingled shock and immense relief, he burst out laughing.

Astonished almost as much as I had been thirty seconds earlier, there was a second or two when I had no idea how I should react, and then it came to me; I smiled, and then I laughed along with him. 'Now get down from there, you little madhead!' I admonished, still grinning. 'And put your pathetic excuse for a knife back as well!'

Incredibly, he did both things without a murmur.

I still felt shaky, and also slightly stunned by what had happened. Who'd have thought I'd end up diffusing a dangerous situation by using a line out of *Crocodile Dundee*?

We did manage to talk about what happened, in the end. Seizing the initiative – and what felt like at least a version of the upper hand – I then changed my mind and suggested he might like to help me, and put the knife to better (and slightly less terrifying) use by chopping some tomatoes and cucumber for a salad. After all, I pointed out, if he loved food so much, it made sense for him learn how to feed himself properly. I even pointed out, remembering Mike's words about Justin's view of 'women's work', that some of the best chefs in the world had started out by helping in the kitchen, just like this. And as we worked, and I felt it safe to broach it again, I talked about the different jobs that people had to do: some people were chefs, other people were policemen, and some people – me and Mike being a good example – had decided to make their job one of helping children. Children like him who had had bad things happen, and who needed lots of love and care to help them feel better about things.

I explained again about the reality of my situation; that as his carer, I worked with other people, and had rules I had agreed to, and one of those rules was that I mustn't keep secrets. Just like chefs had to obey all sorts of rules about hygiene in the kitchen, so that the people who ate their food didn't get sick, so I had to follow the rules I had been given. Which weren't put there to hurt him – absolutely the opposite. I had people who were there to support us – us *and* him – but who could only do so if I told them the truth. Which meant I had no choice – none at all – but to do as I had done. ˙

He seemed to digest all this, nodding at intervals as he stood and chopped beside me, and I felt so much happier that he'd taken it on board now. Even so, I wasn't stupid, and knew he still felt hurt and betrayed. You could be given all the explanations in the world, after all, but you couldn't just conveniently switch your feelings off, could you?

'And there's nothing you can do about it,' Mike reminded me that night, as once again I lay in bed, fretting. 'All you can do is to keep doing what you're doing, love. You've made progress. He'll get over this blip. You'll *keep* making progress.'

'You think so?' I really hoped so, but I wasn't convinced. Maybe it was just too late for Justin.

'I *know* so,' Mike said. 'Look, love. Try to look at it this way. The fact that he felt betrayed – and he will get past that, I honestly do believe that – is precisely *because* he's made progress. It's precisely because he's bonded with you; with all of us, with the family, that this – well, this reality check, if you like – has hit him so hard. Must be *bloody* hard, when you think about it, having your life dictated by a bunch of adults who keep turning up and interfering in your business. I don't know ...' Mike shrugged. 'But maybe he'd forgotten about all of that, you know, having got so settled in here. Which he has. He really has.'

'Yeah, and then he gets grassed up. By *me*.'

'Tsk! Listen to you! Case, come on, I *mean* it. You've got to stop this!' He reached an arm out and put it around my shoulder, then pulled me close and hugged me. 'You're doing great. You're a great mum and a brilliant foster mum, too. It'll come right. I promise. It really will.'

I knew Mike talked sense – he always did – that was why I loved him. But it was dispiriting, even so, to see the change now in Justin. Within a day, all the stuff he'd got out and started leaving around his bedroom – books, toys, computer games, the football rug, a couple of the puzzles – had once again been banished to the back of the cupboard, and the blue throw had been reinstated over the bookcase. Once again, the room looked just like a prison cell. Except, if anything, even more spartan.

This time, though, I noticed something else as well. I had nipped in to pick up the laundry a couple of days later and noticed that his TV had been left on. I picked up the remote to turn it off and realised that the cartoon that was playing was in black and white. Thinking that the TV was broken, I called Mike to take a look. 'No,' Mike said, taking the remote from me and pointing it. 'There's nothing wrong with it. Look.' He pressed a button and the colour returned. 'See? You just have to put the colour back on with the remote.' He handed it back to me. 'He's done it before.'

'What, made the television black and white?'

Mike nodded. 'Yes. I've been in before and seen he's done it.'

'But why would he do that?'

Mike shrugged. 'Search me. But then he does do a lot of odd things, doesn't he?'

I shuddered. And maybe this was what he did when he wanted the TV to match his black moods. This kid just seemed to get stranger and stranger.

And also, it looked like, more and more determined to punish the world for what had happened to him by completely refusing to engage with it. Both John and Harrison came to visit, on separate occasions, and though I wasn't present – I couldn't be, because that was not the protocol – they both reported that they'd got absolutely nowhere. Justin had clammed up; draped that blue throw metaphorically over himself, too, his only response to their gentle questions about what he'd told me being a series of stony looks and silent shrugs.

Casey Watson

At least, I thought, at least he would be off to school now. Maybe the change of scenery, the new environment and new people might help. Perhaps he'd even make a friend or two, who knew?

But in that, it seemed, I was probably being seriously naive. He'd been there only a few days when I got a call from the school, one lunchtime.

'Mrs Watson?' a male voice said. 'It's Richard Firth, Head of Year Seven at the high school. I'm calling about Justin Reynolds. I believe you're his foster mother, yes?'

I felt my stomach lurch. 'Yes. Yes, I am. Is everything alright?'

'I'm afraid not,' he said. 'We're going to have to exclude him from school.'

'Oh, no. Why?' I said, mentally saying but not adding the words, *what, already?*

'For throwing another pupil down some stairs.'

Chapter 9

It was a freezing cold day at the end of February, and, looking out of the front window, I saw the cavalry arriving, here for Justin's LAC review.

LAC simply stands for 'Looked After Child', and this meeting, following Justin's distressing disclosures, had already been put in the diary. But given the school incident and subsequent exclusion, the powers that be had decided to flag it up as urgent.

He'd been excluded from school for a week for what he'd done, and I'd been asked to go in for a meeting to discuss things, with both the head teacher and Justin's special needs co-ordinator, Julia Styles. Thankfully, the girl hadn't been hurt, and was just shaken, but given the potential for serious injury in what he'd done, it was felt important that Justin be sent a strong message. He had also been told how easily this could have been a matter for the police. Thankfully, though, that wasn't going to happen on this occasion, as it seemed that the girl's parents had been satisfied that the school had dealt with the matter appropriately.

Neither I nor the school had been able to establish much in the way of background facts, however, it being almost impossible to get anything out of Justin about it, bar repeated grunts about how all the other kids liked to 'wind him up', and how, on that particular occasion, he'd 'just lost it'. I realised that I would just have to accept that I wouldn't ever get to the bottom of this one.

Since then, we'd spent a trying week with Justin at home, who was guarded, withdrawn and generally uncommunicative, as well as feeling the effects of his resultant loss of points, loss of TV and computer time being the worst – so perhaps the most effective – kind of punishment. Irrationally, I felt like I was being punished too. Life was so much harder at home when Justin was unhappy.

But now he was back, and so the way was cleared for the meeting with his care team to finally take place and his package of current measures reviewed. I reminded myself to have my notebook and pen at the ready for the review, as I knew that it was to be an important one and I didn't want to forget anything that might be helpful.

Not that the situation – Justin being absent – was what I'd initially expected. There was something else going to come up at this meeting, I was sure. They'd specifically told me not to even mention it to Justin and said that Janice wouldn't be invited to it, either. This was very unusual; Mike and I had been told during training that the child is *always* present at an LAC review, and, if they still have contact, the child's parent/s or guardian are always invited too. That Justin's mother wasn't to be consulted seemed very odd to me. It just didn't seem right – whatever the circumstances around it – for a child's future, assuming the parent still had legal access, to be discussed without that parent being present.

But even without Janice it was a pretty big meeting. On my doorstep that morning stood a small but robust posse: as well as our link worker John Fulshaw and Justin's social worker Harrison Green, there was Helen King (educational support), Gloria Harris (the reviewing officer), Julia Styles (the special educational needs co-ordinator) and Simon Ellis (the supervisor of our specialist fostering programme). As Mike was at work, last but not least, there was me.

Good God, I thought, counting them one by one over the threshold. *I just hope I've got enough cups.*

'Come in,' I said aloud, as they made their way past me. 'We can talk in the dining room – through there. Door to the left. I'll just go into the conservatory and grab some more chairs.'

I could hear John telling people to make themselves comfortable. Moments later, he'd joined me in the conservatory.

'Sorry, Casey,' he said. 'We're a little mob handed today, aren't we?'

'You're telling me!' I said, passing him the least tatty of my tatty garden chairs. 'Bloody hell, John. You could have warned me we were having a party.'

'Sorry,' he said again. 'Here, let me grab that one as well. It's just that there's some other stuff come up – quite serious stuff – that needs discussing. Hence the big boss being here, and all the others. Go on – you go and start getting some drinks sorted or something. I can take these through and get everyone settled.'

I tutted at John in mock indignation, though, in truth, he was a master at putting people at their ease, and I always felt more secure when he was around. Which was just as well, because these people, all together, were all a little bit intimidating. They didn't mean to be, I was sure, but they couldn't help it. They just *were*. They were the ones who made all the life-changing decisions, whereas I felt very much the little pit pony, toiling at the coal face.

I went into the kitchen and pulled down my large coffee jug and tea pot and, once I'd filled them, I took them into the dining room to sit alongside the assortment of china I'd already taken through; my non-matching milk jug and sugar bowl and mish-mash of different cups. Why would I have matching cups, though? In our family, we all used mugs.

Seeing them all, I felt slightly embarrassed at my lack of taste in such affairs, even so. It was something I'd definitely inherited from my mother; we'd always been a make-do-and-mend kind of family, always able to find a bit to enjoy a nice treat with the children, but not so fussed on wasting money on posh china. But perhaps, now that I was going to be hob-nobbing with the great and the good of social services, I ought to splash out a bit. I made a mental note to buy a matching set of cups, at least, the next time I did the shopping.

No-one else seemed to notice though – or, if they did, it wasn't obvious – and, to my surprise, Harrison leapt up and proceeded to be mother; it was the most animated I'd seen him so far.

It was Gloria – the 'big boss' – who started the ball rolling, by introducing herself and letting us know she'd be chairing the meeting and also taking minutes – this was going to be pretty official, it seemed. She seemed really nice, though, and I found myself warming to her immediately; she had a friendliness about her, and I wondered what her background might be. She seemed both warm and wise: a reassuring combination. Which was important, as over the last few days, and amid all recent the trauma, I was beginning to find a sense of maternal protectiveness growing inside me. I felt professionally responsible – which I was: Mike and I both were, of course – but now also emotionally responsible for Justin's welfare.

The next stage was for everyone present to give an update to the others about their contact with Justin and his current condition. John confirmed that he'd been unable to glean anything further concerning the disclosures I'd recently passed on to him. Harrison did likewise – he had no notes with him, but said pretty much the same as John had; no further progress.

Julia did have news: she was able to update us about the recent school exclusion. She was able to confirm what the school had told me, that the girl's parents had decided not to take the matter further; but added that as the girl had told the school that she was still frightened of Justin – as were several other pupils – it had been decided that Justin be supervised at break times and lunchtime. He wasn't happy about this, apparently, but they were going to stand firm – it would continue for the foreseeable future.

Helen had more positive news. Apparently Justin's behaviour in class had improved slightly, as had the level of his academic accomplishments. As a result they'd decided to reset his school targets in order to make him push himself even harder, the key to an improving profile being very much grounded in the child constantly striving to do better. They believed this particularly applied to Justin, as they felt that, academically, he had much more to offer than anyone had originally thought, which was pleasing.

It was then my turn and I spent some time describing in detail the distressing disclosures, the discovery of self-harming and the blow-up following Justin finding out I'd passed it all on. I felt strongly, and said so, that though we'd come through it and were okay now, that he was still quite distressed at having to deal with the feelings that confronting these suppressed memories had evoked.

Gloria nodded her agreement. 'I think you're absolutely right, Casey,' she said. 'This is a pattern we see regularly with abused and damaged children. It all comes out and, well … then, sadly, we see what we've seen.' She consulted her notes. 'Anyone got anything else to add here? I see that you've something, John, yes? Some information from one of the younger siblings' social worker?'

I felt my stomach shift. So here was that 'something else' I'd been expecting.

John cleared his throat. 'Yes, and I only got the phone call confirming all the details this morning, so what I've discovered will be news to all of you, I think. But, yes, a colleague rang me to inform me that Mikey – he's the older of Justin's two younger brothers – has given a teacher at his primary school cause to believe that he's been subjected to sexual abuse.' He paused to let all of us take this news in. The implications, if so, were very serious – particularly, I realised, with an already sinking heart, for poor Justin himself.

John continued. 'He apparently told his teacher that his mum's "friend" had been "pulling on his winkie" and that he "didn't like it". And of course, since this fits in with what Justin's told Casey about similar occurrences involving drug dealers in the past, we've alerted the child-protection team. They're obviously investigating it as a matter of urgency because if she still has relationships with any of these characters, then the two boys are obviously at risk.'

'So contact for Justin needs to be suspended, then,' Gloria said.

John nodded. 'Yes, of course. Certainly while all this is going on.'

'Which is going to be tough on him,' I said.

'I appreciate that,' Gloria answered, smiling at me sympathetically.

'And what about the other boys?' I asked. 'Will they be taken into care too?'

'Too early to say,' she said. 'Depends what the child-protection team discover. All I can tell you for sure at the moment is that Mikey, Alfie and Janice are all very much under the microscope.'

'But whatever happens, it's going to impact badly on Justin. Seeing his little brothers is such an incredibly big thing for him. If he's denied that …'

'Well, we'll just have to keep everything crossed that doesn't have to happen,' soothed Gloria. 'But don't worry in any case – whatever happens with the siblings in relation to their mother, we'll make sure they can remain in contact with Justin. We'd obviously make that a priority.' She glanced at her notes and shook her head slightly. 'And from what I've read, the relationship with his mum is pretty frac-tured in any case.'

Not half as fractured, I thought privately, than it would surely become if Janice found out that Justin had disclosed details of the abuse he had suffered and the part it was about to play in the current investigation. If the interven-tion by social services meant she lost her younger sons, she'd blame him. Of that I was sure. However peripherally his own past was a factor compared to the disclosures made by Mikey. However morally wrong and muddle-headed that position might be.

I thought sadly of the contact they had at the moment, which amounted to one phone call to Janice every week. He barely spoke to his little brothers – there'd be the odd time they'd come to the phone, but it wasn't often – and the calls (still, despite everything, a highlight of Justin's week) were absolutely heartbreaking to listen to. The halting conversations, the banality of the subject matter, the lack of anything approaching meaningful, much less loving, communication ... if you didn't know, you could easily be forgiven for thinking that he was trying to make conversation with a stranger on a bus.

It seemed so screamingly clear to me that Justin's most deep-rooted problem – in the here and now of his current life – was not just the trauma of what had gone before, painful though that all was, but the soul-sapping reality of continued rejection by the person who was supposed to love him unconditionally for all time. His mother. His mother, who did not love him at all, it seemed to me. Who had decided at age five that he was some sort of monster. And God only knew what would happen if she lost her other boys. It was too terrible a prospect to even contemplate.

'No, the main thing now,' Gloria said, 'in light of the new information is for us to pull together and support Justin the best way we can. Simon?' She turned to the fostering programme supervisor, who'd up to now said very little. 'You're going to run through this for us, aren't you?'

'Absolutely,' he said, moving his coffee cup to one side and opening a file he'd brought with him. I liked Simon, as did Mike. He'd been one of our assessors during our foster training. He was a no-nonsense Liverpudlian with a real warmth about him, and what seemed a really genuine desire to help the kids. He was also one of those rarities within the system who would cut corners if he had to, bypass the red tape, even at the risk of landing himself in deep water.

'My feeling,' he said now, 'is that Justin could really benefit from some extra, one-on-one contact from one of our support workers, Sandie, the idea being that they can begin meeting once a week, and hopefully build a relationship, gradually, that will take him through into his next mainstream foster placement –' he glanced at me here – 'which is obviously still the ongoing plan. The hope is that she'll become someone he trusts and can talk openly to, of course.'

I took all this on board, and John and I exchanged glances. The idea was that, as foster carers, we became very close to the situation and, in being so, our job was to act as parents, not counsellors. We'd been told that as such we should play 'mum and dad' and leave the professional therapy to the professionals. I absolutely understood the thinking, but, as Simon knew, because we'd discussed it during training, I didn't necessarily agree with it. As parents, we all take on many roles with our own children, and I felt – as did Mike – that the same logic applied; there was no reason why foster care couldn't be simply an extension of this.

But whatever the arguments about the boundaries between parent and counsellor, this was extra support and friendship for Justin, and that could never be a bad thing. I nodded and gave Simon a quick smile.

He smiled back. 'We're also going to allocate a skills worker to him. Someone who can take him out and about into the wider community, and hopefully engage his interest in some new hobbies and team activities, as a means of helping him form proper friendships.'

I really did like the idea of this because, right away, I could see how much Justin would get from this extra, focussed-on-fun-instead-of-talking kind of attention. He'd be excited, I knew, and I'd enjoy telling him about it.

'So there you have it,' Simon finished. 'Let's hope it reaps some benefits. At the very least, if we can continue to make progress with his schoolwork, and all things social, he's definitely moving in the right direction.'

Twenty failed placements already, I thought. And now a child-protection investigation for his mother, to boot. Could it really be that simple to make progress? I wasn't sure I believed that, but I truly hoped so.

The meeting was adjourned soon after, and everyone started preparing to leave, but John, I noticed, didn't put on his jacket.

'Couple of things to tell you,' he said, as everyone filed back out through the front door. 'Any chance of another cup of tea?'

We went back into the kitchen, John carrying the tray of crockery, and I set about re-filling the kettle.

'I've tracked down one of Justin's previous social workers,' he said, joining me at the sink and transferring cups and saucers to the dishwasher for me. 'He's retired now, so I went and paid him a visit personally. Just to see if there was anything else I could dig up.'

I rinsed out our mugs ready for a fresh brew. Him tea, and me my drug of choice, another coffee. 'And?' I said.

'And I think the consensus is that Justin's been telling you the truth. It's pretty much the exact same thing he told this chap back then. Back when he was … oh, about six or seven.'

'But that wasn't on his file,' I pointed out.

John shook his head. 'No, you're right, it wasn't. Seems this chap at the time pretty much dismissed it.'

'Dismissed it? What, all that stuff about performing oral sex on the drug dealer? About the dog? About setting the house alight? He was *five*. Why would he lie about something like that? God, could there have *been* a greater cry for help?'

'I know.' John frowned. 'But apparently – and I quote – he just "thought he was being fanciful". Told me he was always lying. And used to say a lot of stuff that was obviously untrue, like when – aged 5 – he beat up his mum's boyfriend with a pool cue, and how he used to smoke cannabis and so on.'

I tried to picture Justin the little boy and this notion of him 'always lying', and how risky a business it was to just assume something like that. I wasn't naive – I knew better than to believe everything children said, but, still, there is a difference between a kid telling you that he beat someone up in a fight, and the other kinds of horrible things that Justin had disclosed. It didn't take a genius to realise that a child of five wouldn't know such things. Not unless he had actually witnessed them.

I was so sad. How different might his future have been if he'd been properly listened to when he was still young enough to benefit from someone actually believing him? Instead, it seemed, it hadn't even been recorded. He'd already, it seemed, been given up on. 'But I'm still on it,' John promised, as the kettle boiled. 'I'll keep you posted.'

And John had obviously meant what he'd said, for there was more. That lunchtime, not an hour after he'd left, an email came through:

Casey, just thought you should know I have located some more old files relating to Justin. They had been boxed up and stored away on one of the occasions that he was living back with his mum. It seems that when he was taken back into care, the old material, for some strange reason, didn't appear with his new records!!! Honestly, heads should roll for this but probably won't. Anyway, when Justin was seven he was placed with a single carer in her 30s. Coral Summers. She had two young children of her own, a girl of 5 and a boy of 6. Justin had been with them for just two months when Coral requested that he be immediately removed. Apparently he had taken a lighter and got the six-year-old to help him hold down the little girl whilst he started to burn her. Coral heard her daughter screaming and found the three of them in Justin's room. I don't want to alarm you but as I delve further into this, I am beginning to think that this lighter thing is starting to look as though it is a common thread throughout his past, which would seem to further corroborate what I said further. I will let you know if I uncover anything else. *Speak to you soon, JF*

This new information, strangely, didn't faze me at all. If anything, it simply cemented my determination to stop this damning cycle – this business of everything Justin said about the horrors of his early childhood seeming to fall on deaf ears. Challenging though he must have been to deal with – I recalled again those twenty failed placements – I simply couldn't understand why there'd been no continuity in caring for him. Except perhaps it wasn't so difficult to understand why. He'd been shunted back and forth, from care home, to foster home, back to his mother's home, endlessly, and it seemed that at no point had anyone taken responsibility for addressing the root of his problems. At no point had anyone even heard alarm bells, and stopped to ask themselves why.

Justin was damaged because of the things that had happened to him when he was too young to make any sense of them. Then damaged further by an assumption – be it for whatever reason, perhaps no reason – that the problem, at every stage after that, *was* him.

Well, no more, I thought. From here on in, no more.

When Justin got home from school that afternoon I had already prepared a tea of crumpets and hot chocolate – his favourite – for us both. And as I boiled the milk and toasted the crumpets I told him about all the new things the agency had decided to put in place. How he'd have a couple of new friends to take him out for treats and new activities at the weekends; how, because he'd started doing so well at school (both in terms of behaviour and schoolwork, the incident notwithstanding) that they'd set him new, more challenging, targets and, most importantly, because he'd been doing so well with his points – the recent outburst again, notwithstanding – that Mike and I were setting him new targets too.

From now on he'd earn points by doing more complex things, because the day-to-day things that seemed challenging when he came to us, such as behaving nicely at mealtimes and making his bed, were no longer things any of us even thought about any more. From now on he would have to think harder about earning points.

'How?' he wanted to know.

I sat down beside him with the buttered crumpets, and showed him the new list I'd made up that afternoon.

'No more exclusions from school, *obviously*, is at number one,' I said. He smiled ruefully at this.

'And then there's no TV till you've done whatever homework you've got, okay? Three chores around the house every week – but *without* being asked, which is what makes it harder – and being polite all the time, to everyone, both in and out of the house.' I went down the complete list for him as he finished his first crumpet. 'What d'you think, then? You reckon you can manage all of those?'

'Easy,' he said, picking up his mug and grinning at me over it. 'Easy, that lot are, Casey. Piece of cake. Does this mean that my pocket money goes up too?'

I grinned back at him. 'Well, let's just see how you go with your new points first, then me and Mike might have a chat about that.'

I put a second round of crumpets into the toaster to start browning. He seemed genuinely excited about both the new targets and the new provisions. And why wouldn't he be? There were clearly people in the world who genuinely wanted to make his life better. It wasn't rocket science, was it? Of course it pleased him.

In any event, he seemed to have forgotten all about being angry with me. Long may that state of affairs continue, I thought.

Chapter 10

The end of the week saw another email arrive from John Fulshaw:

Hi Casey, I received a call this morning from my manager. He has written to J's last two social workers asking for information to be forwarded urgently. He is waiting for this, but in the meantime he has managed to find out about a couple who fostered Justin two years ago. They are still fostering for us and I have an appointment to see them on Tuesday. I will let you know how that goes when I visit you at the end of the week. Speak soon, JF

I was so pleased that John seemed to be making such an effort to discover all the details of Justin's past for us. It really seemed to me that this was crucial to making further progress with him; it was a cliché, but I felt understanding where he'd come from was the key to helping him find a brighter future.

And what a complicated past it was turning out to be. At the end of that week, when John came for the promised visit – we'd arranged for him to come back so the two of us could do a quick follow-up on the LAC meeting – his expression told me he'd more to impart.

'I have more news,' he said, without preamble, as I showed him in. 'Though brace yourself, because it's not very edifying, I'm afraid.'

'Go on,' I said, as we went into the kitchen. 'I'm pretty much braced for anything, to be honest. I take it it's not the kind of information you'd have been thrilled to pass on before we agreed to have him?'

'You got it,' said John. 'Hit the nail on the head, Casey.' And it turned out he was right. If we'd known it, we might well have acted differently.

He'd been to see the couple earlier in the day, as he'd planned to, and it turned out they'd had Justin for six months a couple of years back; at the time he left them Justin had been nine. They told John that for the first few weeks things had been fine, that they'd all got on and that he'd settled very well.

The placement had followed a period when he'd been living back with his mother, truncated when she'd decided to place him back into care so she could 'concentrate on her new boyfriend'. I felt my hackles begin to rise as John recounted what had happened. How could a mother do that? It was one thing to be in extremis and not coping;

quite another to pick up and discard your own flesh and blood just because you decided they were annoying you. But she'd been able to do it that first time, hadn't she? And if you've done something once, however shocking that something is, you get acclimatised; it's not quite so shocking the next time, and little by little, in this case, it seemed, she had perhaps come to see social services and voluntary care orders, in a drug-addled way, as simply an extended form of childminding.

But at the same time, for Justin, this was a brutal betrayal. Hurt and rejected, he had refused to have contact with his mum following this, perhaps (to my mind) to punish her for sending him away, perhaps in the hope that she'd change her mind. But after three months he relented and asked his carers if he could see her again, and she agreed on two hours every two weeks. Two whole hours – what a generous mother she was, I thought grimly.

It was around now that his mood took a turn for the worse; he became sullen and defiant and withdrew into his shell, telling the couple that his mum loved him and wanted him back but that social services wouldn't let her have him.

Once again, I felt my anger rise as John recounted what they'd said; that when they investigated, Janice did confess that that was what she'd told Justin, because she didn't want him 'knowing that she didn't want him back'.

I'll bet. I thought grimly. *Need a scapegoat to let you off the hook? Try social services. They'll be happy to carry the can.*

'So what happened next?' I asked John, as I poured milk into our drinks. 'Was he told the truth in the end?'

'Yes,' he said, nodding. 'Several times, over the years, I believe. But Justin, of course, refused to believe it. On the couple of occasions when he did confront his mother it would, I'm told, invariably end up in a screaming match, with her inevitably insisting that all social workers were liars, who only wanted to split up families. She'd then come grovelling to social services, apologising for it, but still maintaining that she'd done it because she didn't want to hurt him by telling him the real truth. Bloody awful either way, don't you think?' He sipped his coffee. 'And Justin's subsequent behaviour on this occasion – understandably, I'd say – got worse and worse, culminating in him being excluded from his primary school. He apparently went wild one morning, completely out of the blue, and ended up smashing two computers. It took three staff members to restrain him. And then Janice decided she'd had enough of him too, and suspended contact again, for two months.'

'That poor boy … and this was meant to teach him a lesson?'

'Exactly. And, as you can imagine, when his foster mother broke *this* news, he took it very, very badly; she'd expected that, of course, but not quite the extent of it – not at all. He went into a complete rage and attacked her with a screwdriver, apparently, hitting her with it and threatening to stab her.'

'Oh, God …'

'I know. Bloody wretched, isn't it? Anyway, they never managed to get the relationship back on track again and a couple of months later they felt there was nothing more they could do for him. So he was transferred back into a children's home.'

He paused again, to munch on a biscuit.

'God,' I said, shaking my head as I let it sink in. 'It's just so heartbreaking, isn't it? At every turn it seems to get worse. You really have to wonder if his life wouldn't have been so much better if she'd just rejected him outright and allowed him to move on. Surely that would have been better in the long term than this repeated cycle of hope and then rejection?' John was nodding. 'But the poor kid,' I went on. 'Those two little brothers. It's just so bloody wretched to think just how much he clearly loves those little ones, yet he's been forcibly separated from them for more than half his life.'

'You're spot on, Casey,' John said. 'The word "damaged" really doesn't do it justice, does it?' And there's more.'

'More information?'

He nodded. 'I tracked down another care worker this week too – Mona. She worked in a children's home Justin spent time in. Still does, in fact. Anyway, he was there for a year or so when he was about seven.'

'So just before he got fostered.'

John smiled ruefully at me. 'Pass. There may have been another placement in between. I don't know. Could have been back with his mum, even, for a time. But Mona said they were actually pretty close for a while. Well, she *thought* so; she said he struggled to make attachments to anyone, really, but she liked to think she'd broken through to some extent.

'Anyway, seemed it all went pear shaped; there was this incident. Another child in the home – a boy, couple of years younger – complained that Justin had been burning him with a lighter. And as he had the burns to prove it, Mona obviously followed it up. Had to question Justin, naturally, and the thing that really got to her was his reaction to being questioned – apparently it really scared her. She said he may have been only a young child, but that there was something about his expression – well, you already know, Casey – you've seen it, and you've described it. Well, it worried her. Really made her uneasy. Anyway, he called her 'a fat bitch' and apparently challenged her to prove it, which of course, she couldn't, and that was that.

'Anyway, the upshot was that he never spoke to her again. Not once. Though she said he'd always smile sweetly at her in passing. She'd never forget him, she told me – and I think she's feeling for you now. You know what her last words were?'

'Go on, John – surprise me.'

'That he's a newspaper headline waiting to happen.'

John's words – or rather Mona's – stayed with me all day. Kept me awake that night and still sat on my shoulder the next morning. It had been a spine-tingling moment, sitting there in my kitchen with John. I'd always had that sense that Justin was the human equivalent of a simmering pot, always about to boil over. Had had it since the first time we ever met him, even before he came to live with us. Now, though, armed with all this new information, I didn't just have my gut instinct confirmed, I also knew that when the explosions came, they were likely to be of more volcanic proportions.

But it wasn't just a case of dealing with the straightforward venting of Justin's simmering anger. The damage to him was deep and the manifestations of it were highly complex, as I was to find out, only a couple of days later, for myself.

We'd been really pleased, the following week, to see some evidence of Justin seemingly beginning to fit in more with his peers – he'd been talking a bit about a boy he'd befriended, whose name was Gregory and who apparently had some challenges of his own to deal with; he had learning difficulties, or so Justin informed us, and lived with his aunt, as his mother 'couldn't cope with him'.

We'd already met Gregory a couple of times as he and Justin had started walking home from school together, along with his aunt, and he would sometimes invite them to call into our house for a drink and a biscuit on the way. I got on well with Aunt Jennie, and the two of us had shared a couple of coffees together whilst the boys had half an hour on the PlayStation. She never outstayed her welcome and I was happy that Justin seemed to have made a friendship that was lasting beyond the usual week or two.

I wasn't too surprised, then, when one day Justin burst through the door after school and started to plead with me for Gregory to come over for a sleepover.

'Oh, please,' he begged. 'Can Greg sleep at our house this Saturday? He's asked his auntie and she said it's okay if you say so. Oh, please, Casey. Please say he can.' But though I might not have been surprised, I was also unsure. A sleepover was quite a big thing for us to contemplate, and was also something that could be construed as a 'reward' on his programme, for which he would need to earn points.

Plus he hadn't known Gregory that long yet. 'I don't know, love,' I said, to give myself time to discuss things with Mike, and maybe John. 'You've not known each other long, and your room isn't that big, and ...'

'Oh *please* Casey,' he interrupted, eyes wide, looking hopeful. 'I'm *begging* you. We could easily make a bed up on my floor.'

He looked so sincere, and so excited at the prospect, that my resolve started to weaken immediately. 'Okay,' I said. 'No promises, but here's what I'll do. If you ask Greg to get his aunt to call me tomorrow, so we can have a chat, then maybe – just maybe, mind – we could give it a try.'

Saturday came and along with it the sleepover, which, following various chats and some hard thinking, we had now agreed could take place. I had spoken to Jennie, who had filled me in a little more about Greg. He had attention deficit hyperactivity disorder (ADHD), she told me, and was on medication, but that wasn't anything I couldn't deal with. I'd also spoken to Mike, and had a quick word with John, and we'd all agreed that this would be a good opportunity for Justin to develop his social skills. And this was something that so far, he seemed keen to impress us with – since I'd told him I'd consider it, he'd been a model of good behaviour, tidying his room and repeatedly promising that I wouldn't have to lift a finger or get anything organised; he would do absolutely everything.

And true to his word, he did just that, making up the bed on his floor by himself, and then, once Greg had arrived and settled in, not only showing him how to work one of his PlayStation games, but also allowing him to play with his precious toy soldiers. I smiled as I served them a special fish and chip supper. I needn't have worried, I realised. He was doing himself proud.

But perhaps I should have listened to my instincts more keenly, and been a little slower to relax. It was around eleven in the evening when I heard what sounded like a scream, coming from Justin's room.

'Did you hear that?' I asked Mike, reaching automatically for the remote, so I could check if my ears were working right. We were nearing the end of a movie by now and all had been quiet since I'd gone up to tuck them in at around ten, having allowed an extra half-hour with the lights and TV on.

'I definitely heard something,' Mike confirmed, getting up. 'I'll go and check. They're probably just messing about.' He headed off, seeming largely unconcerned, which was reassuring. 'You'll have to tell me what I missed when I get back.'

Two minutes later, however, I was far from reassured to hear Mike's voice from upstairs too – I could tell he was shouting. I leapt up to go and join him and really give the boys what for. I should have known they'd play up at some point.

But what greeted me was not 'playing up' in any normal sense. I entered the bedroom to find Justin standing at the side of his bed, with a very strange look on his face. It took me a few moments to process what was happening. Mike was kneeling on the floor close by, glaring at him, and it was then that I noticed that Gregory was huddled beneath a duvet on the floor between them. I could hear Gregory sobbing and groaning from inside it, clearly reluctant to give it up, while Mike was trying to prise it from around him.

'What the hell is going on?' I said, looking from Mike to Justin. Justin simply stared at me, his features hardening. 'Mike?' I persisted.

'I don't know exactly,' he said, turning to me. 'But I think he's hurt Greg in some way.' He pointed his finger at Justin as he spoke. 'That's all I know, because neither of them will tell me. All I've managed to get out of Greg is that Justin's really hurt him and that he wants to go home to his auntie. 'C'mon mate,' he said, giving another gentle tug on the duvet. 'Let's get you out of there and see how you're doing.'

I got down on my knees and put my arms around Greg through the duvet. 'It's okay sweetheart,' I said gently as Mike moved aside to make room. Perhaps he'd respond better to a female voice. 'Let's just have a look at you, eh? Then we can phone your Auntie Jennie.'

Greg slowly peeked out now, sobbing loudly. 'J … J … Justin b … b … burned me, Casey. He's a big meanie and he should have a smack. I want Auntie Jennie to come.' His sobs began to grow even louder. 'I want her to come and make me better!'

He was clearly very traumatised and I was devastated. I'd been so full of hope, and felt badly let down. What on earth had Justin done to the poor kid? 'Justin!' I snapped, 'Tell me what you've done to Greg, you hear me!'

I don't know what it was about the tone of my voice, but it seemed to finally shock him into talking. 'I just wanted to see what would happen,' he said plaintively. 'That was all, Casey, honest. I just thought it would be interesting to see!'

'*What* would be interesting?' I barked at him.

'What the wax did.'

I felt alarm bells ringing. '*Wax*? What wax?'

'In the tea-light,' he said. 'The wax in the tea-light!'

It turned out, then, through a series of halting half-sentences, that what Justin had decided would be 'interesting' would be to witness what would happen if he melted a candle – he'd taken both some matches and a tea-light from the kitchen, he admitted – and poured the hot molten wax onto Gregory's skin.

'I didn't think it would *hurt* him,' he protested. 'I only wanted to peel it back off when it set.'

I was both speechless and furious with him, and Mike was livid. He could barely look at, let alone speak to, Justin, as he picked Gregory up to carry him downstairs.

'Get to bed, young man,' I told him as I followed Mike out. 'Not a peep – we'll be dealing with you in the morning!'

I then had the unenviable task of phoning Jennie and explaining to her what had happened. It was almost midnight by now, and I felt awful that she had to rush around at this hour. She wouldn't hear of us driving Gregory home ourselves, since we didn't know the way, so she had to come out herself – probably the last thing she expected – to collect her frightened and traumatised nephew.

Worst of all was that, seeing how upset we both were, she made it clear that we mustn't feel in any way responsible. She knew, she said, that Gregory was a vulnerable child, and blamed herself for allowing him to sleep out.

The next day we went through the usual sanctions with Justin. No privileges, no TV and no PlayStation. Not much of a punishment for most kids, I imagine, but to Justin, such losses were torture.

But about the motivation behind his own form of 'torture' I was ambivalent. It had really seemed that he had no notion of the pain he'd inflicted, and I wondered if he was so used to extreme pain himself, via his bouts of self-harming, that he genuinely didn't think he'd hurt Gregory that much. It was either that, or that he *did* know, which made for an equally depressing picture.

Either way, it was a wake-up call for both of us. Not to mention being a stark reminder of Mona's chilling prophecy.

* * *

But incidents such as this, I mused, once my initial shock had died down, were *exactly* what our kind of fostering was about. It may have been shocking to see what had previously been just a set of notes actually happening in our midst, but this was why I'd wanted to do it so badly in the first place. This – this whole tapestry of tragedy heaped on tragedy, and all the far-reaching ramifications – was exactly what drove Mike and I. I just hoped we could unpick all the bad threads that were making a muddle of the rest, and so succeed where so many others had failed. But I knew now, more than ever, that this would be a tall order. A real challenge. Justin seemed more complex by the minute.

'Curry or pizza or Chinese – what's your preference?'

It was the following Saturday morning and Mike and Kieron were off to football as per usual. It had been a quiet sort of week since all the revelations and rearrangements, but, even so, I felt shattered and not at all like cooking a big family dinner. Tonight I had a date with a take-away and the telly and someone else would definitely be doing the washing up.

'Curry!' Mike, Kieron and Justin all said together, though Justin's contribution came from the behind the PlayStation controller that he was, as ever, feverishly play-ing on. Indeed, today, having only just got his privileges back, he was even more obsessed with it than usual. One day, perhaps, we'd get him off to football with the boys, but today wasn't the day, I thought, to push it.

It had been much colder than usual, with a bitingly chilly wind, and I was actually happy to spend the day indoors myself, my scheduled mooch around the shops with Riley having been cancelled a little while back because she'd been feeling a bit off-colour. I did miss my daughter, though, and felt a little redundant as I dragged the mop and bucket out from the cleaning cupboard.

She'd said she might pop round later and, if not, I might stroll down to hers, but it was probably a good thing for me to catch up with a bit of housework and cleaning in the meantime; I'd forgotten, and had been forcibly reminded by having Justin, that having an extra person in the house created a lot of extra dust. And I definitely couldn't be having that.

'That's a shame,' I said, grinning. 'Because I fancy Chinese …' I pushed my sleeves up. 'Only kidding. Now get out from under my feet. And you, Justin,' – I paused here, to look at my watch – 'have only forty-seven minutes of TV time left before I stage a takeover of the sofa and remote!'

I'd planned, as is my slightly obsessive way with house-work, on making a circuit of the upstairs bedrooms, stripping beds as I went, before embarking on a big upstairs dustathon. And since Justin's was the first door on the left once up the stairs, it seemed logical to tackle that room first.

It was, as it had been for a little while now, a mess, but in a good way. Since the last time he'd stripped it back to basics, he'd now got most of his belongings out again.

There was dirty washing piled up in a heap behind the door, DVDs and cases strewn around the floor, and the carpet was actually a small sea of toy soldiers, which looked like they'd originally been set up in ranks but were now, given that they were mostly lying prostrate all over the place, in the last throes of some important battle or other, during which almost all of them had been slaughtered.

I crossed the room, casually dispatching a further couple of gallant heroes, and pushed my sleeves up, ready to get stuck in. As I approached the bed, however, something caught my eye immediately. On it was Justin's memory box, which, along with his photo album that he kept in it, was open.

We'd learned about memory boxes during our training. Lots of kids in care have them apparently. In an uncertain world and with, very often, equally uncertain futures, they are encouraged to keep a tangible store of cherished memories, so they have touchable reminders of happy times. As well as photographs of loved ones, greeting cards and letters, a box might also include things like ticket stubs from the cinema or a sporting event, programmes, souvenirs, postcards – anything, really, with something meaningful about it, that they could look through when feeling sad or lonely.

I had seen Justin's memory box several times already, but he had always been looking in it and, invariably, he would close it if anyone approached. Where he kept it, I didn't know, because he secreted it away, and though I'd been through his room thoroughly when I'd tracked down his stash of socks, I hadn't seen it, and, in any case, hadn't wanted to intrude. These things were clearly private, and I respected that, obviously, though I was very keen to have him open up to me more, and things like this would prove very helpful. I had asked him a couple of times if he wanted to go through the box with me, but he'd always shaken his head and gone, 'Nah, there's nothing in there. It's just crap', or something equally dismissive. And though he would sometimes bring photographs from the box to show us, the actual box always stayed put.

Yet here it was now, just sitting on his bed, wide open, almost as if he'd put it there specifically for me to find. Engrossed as he'd been on the games console when I'd left him, he knew perfectly well that I was coming upstairs to clean bedrooms.

It just seemed way too much of an open invitation to resist, particularly since the incident with Gregory – so, spurred on by the knowledge that the more I knew about him the better I could help him, I sat down on the bed and placed it on my knees.

It was a shoebox, that had been transformed by being encased in black faux-leather, and was covered in Bart Simpson stickers. In the centre of the lid there was a small photograph of Justin aged around eight years old, though it was difficult to make out as the box and lid had obviously been reinforced often; both were criss-crossed with many layers of Sellotape.

Inside was a menu from a Tex Mex restaurant, some birthday cards, a brochure from a theme park and a football programme, plus a number of different kinds of sea shell. There were also lots of photos, some of children – who I assumed were his little brothers, because I could see a definite family likeness. Not that I knew just how much of a family likeness, because, as with Justin, their paternity was unknown, none of her 'boyfriends' sticking around for long enough to lay claim to them. Justin had asked his mother, apparently, some years back, but had been simply told not to be nosey.

The photos also included ones of a variety of women, all of which (not just the dark-haired ones, this time, I noticed) had had their faces stabbed with something sharp and their eyes carefully removed. It looked like it had mostly been done with scissors. Most heartbreaking of all was that so many were crumpled; the ones of his mother particularly badly, as if they'd not only been stabbed at repeatedly, but then also been screwed up in distress many times.

And then – and I felt my eyes smart at this – smoothed out again. At least, in so far as they could be. It was a record of the many times in his young life he'd felt unloved, and then loved, and then abandoned, and then hopeful. It was very, very difficult to look at.

And it seemed I wasn't the only one looking.

I don't know how much time had passed when I first became aware of it, but while I was sitting there deciding I must press Justin to talk to me about this, I suddenly had that feeling that I was no longer alone. I looked up then and, sure enough, he was standing in the bedroom doorway.

He said nothing at all, just crossed the room towards me, took the box, closed it and calmly placed it under his pillow.

For all his silence and his uncharacteristic lack of histrionics, I could feel his anger thrumming in the air. I felt a wave of embarrassment and floundered for a moment, feeling I'd been caught redhanded doing something naughty. 'Justin, love …' I began. I … I … was … well, it was just *there*, and –'

'You were looking at my private stuff,' he said calmly.

'I was cleaning love, that's all. And it was there, open, on your bed.'

He stared at me for a moment before shrugging his shoulders 'Don't matter anyway,' he said. 'It's only a load of old crap.'

I stood up, then made myself busy smoothing the duvet. 'I'm so sorry, love,' I said. 'It's your personal things. I really had no right to …'

'It's fine Casey,' he said, and his tone was light, even dismissive. 'I'm just gonna stay in here now, though, if that's okay. And watch a DVD.'

'Yes, yes, that's fine. I can do your room later.'

I hesitated a moment, in case he wanted to say more, but he just turned, knelt on the floor and started gathering up DVDs. So I left the room, quietly closing the door behind me. And though the feeling persisted that he'd *wanted* me to see it, I couldn't help feeling really bad. I had intruded on something personal to him, and that was something I could never have imagined myself doing.

* * *

When I passed his room later, Justin was still in there, only now he was no longer watching a DVD, but once again stripping it of all but its functional furniture, and apparently doing it on autopilot. If he heard me or saw me, he certainly didn't register it. Same process, I thought, but this time without the drama.

I wasn't sure who he was trying to punish; me or himself. It was just such a desperately sad thing to witness.

Chapter 11

April had arrived and with it some slightly warmer weather at long last and, like another ray of sunshine, Riley was on the phone. 'Mum, it's me,' she said, and I could tell right away that she was brighter than she had been of late. Which was good to hear, as I'd been a little worried about her. It wasn't like Riley to be ill – she was almost invariably like a Duracell bunny. But she'd been feeling off-colour more than once in the last couple of weeks. I'd been just about to call her myself.

'Hiyah, lovey,' I answered. 'You feeling better? You certainly sound it.'

'Brilliant, thanks,' she said brightly. 'Just wanted to check you were in.'

'Yes, I am. No plans to be going anywhere, either. Why, are you going to pop round?'

'I was, yes. Mum, what time's Dad likely to be home?'

Strange thing to ask, I thought. 'Usual time,' I answered anyway. 'Around five-ish or so. He didn't say any different when he left this morning. Why?' Mike was a warehouse manager for a big office-furniture supply company. He worked long hours, but, thankfully, also regular ones.

'Good,' she said firmly, but not answering my question. 'I'm just going to wait for David to get back from work, then we'll be over. Can we have tea at yours?'

All these strange questions! But what a daft one this was. 'Of *course* it's okay, stupid! It'll be lovely to see you both. I was just going to do pizza for Justin and Kieron, but I'm sure I can come up with something more elegant for us four. Hey, but listen, you sound like there's some particular reason for all this. I mean, it's lovely to see you *any* time, but –'

Riley laughed. 'That's because there *is* a reason, mum. See you about five-thirty, okay? Byeee!'

But there was no time to dwell on what the reason might be because almost as soon as I'd put down the phone, I heard the front door bang and a spirited 'Hi, Casey!' being bellowed from the hallway, closely followed by the sound of a herd of wildebeest thundering up the stairs. It was Justin, home from school and, as had become his routine now, dashing upstairs to get out of his school uniform.

I let go my breath and simultaneously realised that Justin wasn't the only one who'd got into a routine. Holding my breath on his arrival was mine – at least till I was sure of the mood he was in; sure he wasn't going to kick off and spoil everyone's day. It was ridiculous, and I mentally chastised myself for it. He was an eleven-year-old child, not a monster.

But glancing at the clock I realised there was no time to dwell on that either; if Riley and David were coming to eat with us I needed to think about what it was we *would* eat, and that meant a thorough rummage in the fridge and freezer. I also needed to press on and get Kieron and Justin fed. Whatever impromptu arrangements I fixed up with my daughter, my son wanted feeding when he got in from college and it was also important I stuck to Justin's meal chart; both the timing and the menu were non-negotiable.

Justin himself joined me in the kitchen just as I was taking the pizza out of the oven. It was almost as if he had some sort of sixth sense for knowing exactly when food was going to arrive.

'Just in time!' I quipped. 'Hey, that's what we should call you, shouldn't we? Justin Time!' I was in a buoyant mood knowing Riley and David would soon be over. Justin, too, it seemed. He found this hilarious.

'What's so funny?' asked Kieron, arriving in the door-way. 'Ah, pizza!' he said, seeing it and emitting a small cheer. 'That's good. So I won't die of starvation after all.'

They went through to the dining room with their tea and I could hear them laughing and chatting. This was shaping up to be a good day all round, I decided. I then grabbed a coffee and cleared the desks and set about round two – preparing a nice tea for the rest of us. As it was so summery, I'd settled on cold roast chicken and salad. Mike would probably moan – he was more of a pie and chips man – but oh, well. Didn't matter. It was all food.

Five-thirty arrived and, with it, David and Riley. 'Thank God for that,' Mike said, letting them in and mock-frowning. 'It's bad enough that I'm forced to eat rabbit food after a hard day at work, but even worse to have to wait half an hour for the pleasure!'

'No, no – we can't eat yet!' Riley said, seeing me emerge from the kitchen with the salad bowl. 'You need to get everyone gathered together first, so we can tell you our news. Where's Kieron? And Justin. Dad, can you get them?'

'They're back upstairs,' I said. 'Playing on the computer in Kieron's bedroom. But –'

'Mum, Dad!' Riley chided, while David stood there grinning goofily. 'Stop staring and go get them, will you!'

I took the salad bowl and plonked it back on the kitchen table, while Mike bellowed to the boys to come down. 'Quick, you two!' he added – probably for the benefit of his stomach, while I, meanwhile, had a sudden bolt of inspiration. I looked at Riley, then at David – the pair of them like a couple of grinning idiots. It couldn't be, could it? Or maybe it *could* be …

The boys both thundered down then, Kieron volubly complaining. 'This had better be good, Riley. We were in the middle of an important game!'

But his big sister was having none of it. 'Shut up and sit down, you two,' she ordered, and it was only once they'd done so and she had all our full attention that she deigned to impart their 'big news'. Which *was* big. At least, would before too long become so. 'Everyone,' she announced. 'David and me want you to be the first to know. I'm pregnant. We're going to have a baby!'

Now my heart really *did* leap. So my hunch had been right. This was a shock, but such a great one. Such a fabulous thing. Mike and me were going to become grandparents!

I glanced at Mike to see him looking stunned, his eyes filling up with tears. Then he leapt up from the sofa and the room all but exploded – into a big noisy round of hugs and congratulations, with everyone kissing everyone else, just like it was New Year. But then, minutes later, I noticed Justin, in the corner.

It was his face; it had taken on that strange inhuman quality. He looked like thunder. I could see he was seething.

'You okay, babes?' I asked him quietly, but he seemed unable to answer. In fact, I could see he was struggling hard to try and maintain control. He was shaking, and he looked like he wanted to punch something. Luckily, it didn't seem as if anyone else had noticed, and with me now standing between him and everyone else, hopefully they wouldn't notice, either. I really didn't want this wonderful occasion spoiling.

I discreetly manoeuvred him – and thankfully he didn't try to resist – out into the hallway, and then looked right into his eyes, maintaining contact as I spoke to him. 'Look,' I said gently, but also quite firmly. 'I know something about all this has upset you, Justin, but we don't want to hurt

Riley's feelings, do we? You're obviously too angry to talk to me about it right now, I can see that, so why don't you go on back upstairs for a bit, eh? Kieron will be up in a minute and you can get back to your game. Okay, love?'

For a moment he looked like he was about to speak, but then changed his mind and clamped his mouth shut again. Then he turned and plodded off back up to his bedroom and as I watched him go up, I slowly exhaled. Once again, I'd been holding my breath.

We didn't see Justin downstairs again until Riley and David had finally left for home, and when he did come down, he had Kieron close behind him. And for a reason; when I asked him about it, sensing he was calmer, and would want to talk about it, right away, Kieron, who was standing behind him, was busy making a face at me and shaking his head.

Taking my cue, I dropped it, and instead just ruffled Justin's hair. 'I know it's a lot of fuss, kiddo,' I said lightly. 'But don't worry. It'll calm down soon enough.'

It was only once he'd gone to bed that Kieron told me what had happened. He'd been aware from the off what had happened to Justin, bless him – had actually seen him metamorphose into that other, scary Justin, and though I hadn't been aware of it, specifically popped upstairs to check all was okay.

Once up there, he'd asked Justin if he was okay and, getting little back, then observed, 'Bloody women, eh! Getting all over-excited about babies! So. Back to our game, then? Prepare yourself, mind. Welcome to defeat, little brother!'

Justin had apparently laughed out loud at this, his parting comment on the subject being an equally spirited, 'Hah! She won't be so happy when she's round and fat like my mum!'

I could have kissed Kieron for that. I really could. Trust him to have the wisdom to say *exactly* the thing Justin needed to hear. I really felt proud of him that day.

'It's not really surprising he's found it difficult to swallow,' said Mike, once we were tucked up in bed, him with his book and reading glasses and me with my magazine and coffee, like the grandparents-in-waiting we couldn't believe we now were. 'Hard for him to separate it from what's happened with *his* mum, is it? You know, another woman having a baby, all the fuss and attention and everything. Must remind him of how wretched his own family life is.' Mike put the word 'family' in quote marks with his fingers, and he was right to – what sort of family life was Justin ever going to have? His mother was about as reliable as the British summer. What were the chances of her every really wanting to reconcile with Justin once her 'princess', her precious baby daughter, came along? My guess was that she wouldn't want him within a mile of her.

But all we could do for Justin was what we were doing already – trying to give him stability and boundaries and affection and, as far as possible, help him to deal with the scars he already had. And I couldn't dwell on it all – not that night – as I was way too excited. 'Grandparents'. It made me giggle just to say it out loud. In my head I was way, way too young to be a 'nanna', and I laughed when I realised I was actually rehearsing in my head how I was going to break the news to my parents. How mad was that?

But there was a serious aspect to this incredible new situation; the effect this would have on our fostering. Way in the future, though we'd yet to have so much of an inkling of it, our fostering would turn out to be such a great positive that it would end up having a direct effect on Riley's own choice of career, but for the moment, as Mike commented, we must proceed with caution. We must make sure we had a much fuller background on future children, especially older ones, to be sure they didn't have a history of hurting little ones.

In the meantime, I agreed, thinking about Justin's reaction earlier, we must take care. If he was still with us when the baby was born – it was due in November – we mustn't be blind to how that might affect him.

The days passed, and I never really did get Justin to articulate his difficulty about Riley and her pregnancy. Even though, intuitively, it was so obvious why it affected him, it still would have been so helpful for him to be able to talk his feelings through with me, yet as a subject for discussion, no matter how hard I tried to set things up for him to attempt it, it seemed it was a definite no-go area. I heard second-hand from Kieron that his only other comment to him on the matter was that all girls were 'slags' and that he knew 'all the stuff they do to get pregnant'. He also warned Kieron that he should never get a girlfriend, because they were 'trouble'.

Despite him not opening up about it to me, his distaste was still palpable and obvious, even if it wasn't aggressive. He would simply get up and leave any room Riley entered. Riley herself, blooming and beaming, was philosophic, however. 'He'll get over it, Mum,' she said. 'I know he will. And I'm not taking it personally. So don't worry about it.'

Bless her too, I thought. And she was spot on, of course. If we ignored it, he'd probably get past it all the quicker. In the meantime, we'd just ride it out.

But his reaction to Riley's pregnancy aside, I was beginning to feel Justin and I were making progress again. Relations between the two of us were just beginning to feel so much warmer; I could sense a return of the closeness we'd begun to develop before the massive blow-up following his last disclosures. And by the last day of term, as I prepared the crumpets and the chocolate, I realised our weekly 'points' meetings were something I had begun to look forward to.

They were, however, always bitter sweet. Since he was doing well on level two now, he had quite a lot to spend, and a big part of our 'meeting' was to sit down together so he could decide what he'd like to spend them on.

He didn't tend to deviate a great deal. A third of his points would be used up on the 'basics': an 8 p.m. bedtime, TV and DVD player in his bedroom, time to spend on the computer. He was then meant to use the rest of his points up on various things on the pre-arranged programme manager's list, which included extra peer time or having a pal round for tea. It also, rather poignantly, included 'sleepovers with friends' – something that, since the incident with Gregory and the candle wax, would be out of the question for the foreseeable future. Sadly, if predictably, he'd never do all of them anyway, and instead – without commenting in any way about them – he'd just quickly skip the page altogether. He'd then quickly move on to the things that he could do, like ordering a special take-away, choosing a DVD or game rental, or going somewhere special with either one of us or one of his carers. That he had no friends his own age must have been constantly on his mind – how could it not be? – but he'd always come to the last section as if the things he was choosing were the most exciting imaginable, so it didn't even occur to him to want to have friends.

It was heartbreaking, yes, but there was a positive to it too. He would confide in me again. And today he did.

I couldn't quite pin down what it was that prompted it, but out of the blue, while we were just finalising his treats, he said, 'You know, when I was eight, I went to hospital.'

I put my pen down. 'Really? What for?'

'My mum's boyfriend beat me up,' he said, almost casually. 'He was drunk and he beat me up and I was bleeding an' that, and it was pretty bad, and in the end Mum said I had to go to hospital. But I had to tell them different. I had to tell the doctors and nurses that I'd been riding my bike and I'd, like, crashed into a wall, and I'd gone over the handlebars and that's how I got all the bruises. I had to tell them that I landed in a ditch, and that the ditch was full of stones. Rocks, actually. Yeah, it was rocks they said I had to say.'

I could feel myself blanching at this chilling recall. The little details he'd obviously been carefully schooled to include. Could this be 'fanciful'? As if. I didn't think so for a single instant. Once again, given that this would have been recorded somewhere, I found myself doubly shocked that, periodically, he was allowed to go back and live at home. Surely there was a point when enough was enough? When going 'home' was making everything much worse? I commented on all this to-ing and fro-ing and Justin seemed genuinely shocked I didn't know.

'I went home lots,' he said. 'You know, when she was okay. When she had a boyfriend. But it never worked out. She never kept me. I ran away one time –'

'Did you?'

'Yeah. When she was with that bloke who beat me up. I ran away and I didn't know where to go or nothing, so I ended up sleeping in a skip for two nights.'

'In a skip?'

He nodded. 'Yeah. An' it was horrible. You know, really scary and that. And I kept thinking someone would be out looking for me, you know – police cars. Social services. *Someone*. But no-one came and in the end I went home again.' He scratched his head. I mentally noted that his mop of curls really needed cutting. 'And you know what? When I came home, an' that, you know what she did?'

'No I don't,' I said.

'Nothing. Nothing at all. She just looked up from the TV and she said, "Oh, there you are". And that was it. Then she just said, "Go and see to your brothers", like I never went missing at all.'

I kept my voice and expression light, to match Justin's – he was so matter of fact – as he went on to describe how he used to scavenge in dustbins, to find food for his brothers, and how one time he had to get up very early in the morning so he could go to the woods with one of his mum's boyfriends to help him pick magic mushrooms for all the grown-ups.

Listening to him recount this grim collection of childhood memories, I couldn't help but wonder at how a child could ever hope to come to terms with so much. But when he told me, almost proudly, how he'd been taught how to build a special kind of pipe, for smoking drugs through, describing how you could use a glass milk bottle and a length of hose, it was a real effort of will to stop a red mist from clouding everything.

But I managed. We finished the crumpets and he seemed so happy that we'd chatted. Instead I noted everything down in my journal that evening. My journal that had become something of a friend to me. It had started pristine and empty, a sea of inviting blank pages, but now it was really filling up. It had been supplied to Mike and I by our fostering agency, and had proved to be a really important piece of kit. Leather bound, with our initials and surname embossed in gold in the bottom corner, it looked far too sophisticated for my scrawly notes. But scrawl I did. Even more so on that night. In fact, the longer Justin was with us, the more detailed and elongated my entries had become.

And, very soon, there'd be more.

Chapter 12

Sunshine, I thought happily, as I yanked open the bedroom curtains. I loved sunshine. I loved sunshine almost as much as I loved snow. You could keep all the dull drizzly stuff in between, but give me sun or give me snow, and I'm in over-drive. Which was something I definitely needed to be today. 'Mike! It's sunny!' I said out loud. 'Thank God for that!'

'Yes, thanks for the weather report, Case,' he grunted, squinting. 'I think I can tell that for myself.'

Yes, I needed sun today like I'd never needed it before – so much so that I'd even considered doing whatever the opposite of a rain dance is because in our part of the country, sun – even in early May – wasn't something you could ever rely on. And I needed sun today, particularly, because it was the day of Justin's party. He would be twelve and we were all of us united in the cause of making it a birthday he would never forget.

'Pleeease get up Mike,' I begged. 'Stop snuggling back under that duvet, you old grump – it's party day!'

Mike conceded with a groan and threw back the duvet. 'Okay,' he said, yawning. 'I give in. I know I won't get any peace trying to have a lie in, will I?'

'Absolutely not!' I replied, tutting, as I practically skipped out of the bedroom. Honestly, I thought, men have no idea!

In my case, this was no kind of hardship. As with Christmas, my affection for parties was a constant in my life, and my own children's lives had been punctuated annually with the sort of over-the-top festivities I loved to put on. For Riley, I'd peaked with my '*Grease*' extravaganza, building a 'shake shack' in the garden, making everyone dress in 50s clothes, and having a Frankie Valli lookalike open the party by singing 'Beauty School Dropout' just as Riley walked in.

Kieron, too, had some spectacular birthday bashes over the years, in his case, almost invariably, since he loved comic-book superheroes, involving a giant blow-up Superman or Spiderman scaling the house walls. And now it was Justin's turn to get the full Casey treatment. I couldn't wait to get my teeth into this one.

The preparations for Justin's party had been going on in secret for a couple of weeks now, and I'd taken great care to ensure that he didn't twig. All he knew was that we were going to have a 'little family tea party', with just my niece and nephew coming round to play. It was sobering to see just how excited he was about the low-key event we'd pretended we were putting on for him – clearly the celebration of his own special day had never been a part of his young life. So I couldn't wait to surprise him with the real one I'd dreamed up – in reality, my plans were *way* bigger. I'd invited a couple of my close friends, plus various members of my extended family including my niece and nephew, of course, as they were both around Justin's age. I'd also been in cahoots with Justin's new teaching assistant, Cathy. Because it was to be a surprise, I couldn't ask Justin to invite school friends, so instead, she'd helpfully done some research and identified half a dozen children who Justin seemed to be on good terms with. She did comment that finding more than that would be a pretty tall order, as, given the extent of his emotional problems, he found it difficult to make and keep friends. Still, I thought, with the numbers swelled by the Watson contingent (always enthusiastic party goers, us lot!), I was sure that would be plenty to create a buzz.

I was already buzzing with ideas for it, for sure. We all were. Since *The Little Mermaid* was one of Justin's favourite Disney films, we'd decided to theme his party around that; our plan was to completely transform the back garden as a sort of 'undersea kingdom', complete with beach, swimming pool and lots of themed decorations. Both Kieron and Riley had been a great help in all this, spending hours with me making all the things that we needed. I was so proud of them both – they had leapt upon the project with genuine enthusiasm, and seemed as keen as I was that we'd make the day as special as we could.

Riley had made all sorts of *papier-mâché* sea creatures – starfish and crabs and lots of different kinds of fish – while Kieron had been equally busy with paint and glue and scissors, painting and cutting out lots of giant underwater plant life for us to stick up along the length of the garden fence. He'd also come with me to get a few enormous bags of play sand, so we could make a proper beach, and then there was the *pièce de résistance*, of course. It had been something of a major extravagance, I knew, but the centrepiece of the whole party was a small rigid swimming pool I'd hired for the day. It was eight feet in diameter and an impressive three feet deep, and the company were coming to erect it and fill it later in the morning.

Having thrown open the curtains and treated Mike to a couple of bars of 'Who can Buy This Wonderful Morning' as an extra inducement not to lie and fester, I harried Mike from the bedroom (though he might have called it 'escaping') and asked him nicely to put the kettle on while I showered. I still had a whole load of preparations to get finished, and he needed to get on with things as well. He was supposed to be taking Justin swimming this morning, the trip to the pool and a chance to play on the water slides being what we'd told Justin his main birthday treat was. I hummed to myself as I turned on the shower. I couldn't wait to see the look on his face when he returned and saw what his *real* birthday treat was.

* * *

The day had started well, and I was glad. Mike and I had given Justin new trainers for his main present, together with a PlayStation game he wanted and a selection of DVDs. He'd already had a card from his 'team' with a gift voucher in it, another card with a £10 voucher from his social worker, Harrison, and when the morning post arrived – and about which I'd been fretting very much – another card had come, which he immediately recognised.

'It's from Mum!' he cried, his face alight with joy as he saw it. 'I know it is! I recognise the writing!' He ripped it open while I tried to feel the same sense of enthusiasm. Couldn't she at least have managed a parcel? A surprise? Something for him to open? But no, it was just a card with a tenner in.

'Look, Casey!' Justin shouted excitedly, even so. 'Ten pounds! She has hardly any money and she sent this! And look – my little brothers have both signed it by themselves!' His pleasure was almost palpable; he was just so damned happy!

I'd tried to feel happy for him, too. I *was* happy for him. A child's love for their parent is completely unconditional, and I could see how much this small effort she'd made truly meant to him. But it was hard, because it stuck in my throat. She was his mother – she should want to give her all to her child.

It wasn't the fact that she had only sent money, because I knew that ten pounds had probably stretched her financially. But surely she could have put some thought into spending that money on a small gift, something she knew that Justin could keep and treasure, even put into his memory box? It was so tragic how little real, consistent effort she'd made for her son. And unprompted? The cynical me wondered about that too. Had social services given her a nudge?

Stop it, I'd said to myself. *Just be happy he's so happy.* And very soon – a few hours later – he would be even happier. I had to bite my tongue to stop myself letting on.

An hour later, and having finally seen Mike and Justin off, I thought I'd pop up and have a quick clear of Justin's room. If he was having school friends over – a first – then I wanted him to be able to make a good impression, so I thought I'd have a tidy up, make the bed, have a quick flick round with the duster; just make it look more inviting and free up some floor space.

I had no thought in my head that wasn't party related – why would I? – as I gathered up DVDs and stray toys. He had a box, a plastic crate, in which he kept all his soldiers, and I thought it would be a good idea to put it out of the way, under the bed, along with a couple of other boxes which were taking up floor space. It was while doing so that I came upon the suitcase.

Well, not came upon, exactly, because it had been there from day one. It was the case he'd arrived with, which had held his pitifully few possessions, and it had been stored under his bed from the off. I'd thought it was empty – when I'd discovered all the scissors and blades, it certainly had been – but as I went to move it (I wanted to shove it along a bit, to fit the crate in) it was clear that it wasn't empty now. It was so weighty, in fact, that I was unable to slide it along one handed, so instead I grabbed the handle and pulled it half out. Intrigued now about what could be the cause of its great weight, and with a sudden slight anxiety about what I might find, I pulled it fully out and undid the zip.

The sight that greeted me was an astonishing one. I'm not sure I'd had any idea what to expect, but not in a million years would I have imagined what I did see. The case was full of food. There were literally hundreds of small food items in there, all neatly stacked and sorted in order of shape and size. There were packets of sweets, different chocolate bars, crisps and instant pudding mixes, packets of dried soup; all manner of different kinds of non-perishable foods. None were opened, and there was also a hand-written note sitting on top of them, in which Justin had painstakingly catalogued every item in his big scrawly handwriting. He'd taken care, I noted, even as I sat there, bewildered, to spell carefully and write on the lines.

Apart from that, though, I don't think I had a coherent thought in my head. I simply gawped at it all, unable to believe my eyes. But one thing was clear. They hadn't come from my cupboards. They were budget-range items, own-brand supermarket products, and didn't even come from the supermarket I used. So where had they come from? Had he stolen them from somewhere? And what were they all there for, anyway? This wasn't just a stash of goodies for an impromptu midnight feast. This was strange, and unsettling, this perfectly aligned collection; something like you'd expect to come across in a piece of futuristic fiction – a collection gathered together in anticipation of a nuclear strike; the kind of thing the government might have suggested during the Cold War, along with the advice to stockpile water and to hide under the kitchen table. I looked again at the neatly compiled list that lived with them. What on earth had gone through his mind when he sat and wrote it out? I didn't have the slightest idea.

And I wasn't about to find out. Not right now. I zipped the case back up and replaced it exactly where I'd found it, then went back downstairs to make a start on the party food instead. Today was definitely not the day to confront Justin with what I'd found.

I'd told everyone to get to ours at around one-thirty, if possible, as Mike and Justin were due back around two. By now, in the nick of time, the swimming pool was up and filled, the sunlight glinting prettily off its spangly surface. The beach was in position too, all having been carefully raked over, and Riley and Kieron and I had finished accessorising the garden which, we all agreed, looked pretty amazing. My sister and brother and their families and all our friends had arrived, and everyone was now pitching in and helping out with getting the last preparations finished, as well as keeping an eye on my niece and nephew, to make sure they didn't sneak off and clamber into the pool.

But only one of Justin's friends had come, so far, to my great disappointment. On top of what I'd seen in Justin's bedroom this morning, it was really upsetting, and I'd fretted about it. Then Tarika, the deaf girl who Cathy, the teaching assistant, looked after as well as Justin, told me that the two of them seemed to get on well, and sat and ate lunch together most days.

Tarika, who was a pretty blonde girl with enormous blue eyes, had been dropped off by her parents at 1.30, as agreed, but seemed shy, and stuck to me like glue. I spent the last twenty minutes with one ear tuned to the front doorbell, just in case some more came, but they didn't. I tried to tell myself it didn't matter – one friend was better than no friends, after all – and that as Justin wasn't expecting any, he wouldn't be disappointed, would he?

And as it turned out, perhaps predictably, he was anything but.

'Wow!' he said, eyes wide, as he surveyed his birthday kingdom. 'Wow, Casey! This is just amazing!' He was jumping up and down, clapping his hands, and swivelling his head to take it all in. 'Wow! A barbecue! Oh my God, a *pool*! Oh, this is mint! Mike, I can't believe you didn't tell me!' Mike grinned at Justin's reaction and gave him a quick squeeze around his shoulders. 'Sorry, mate,' he confessed, 'but I was under strict orders.'

I tousled Justin's still damp curls. He was like the cat with the cream. 'All part of the service,' I told him. 'It's your special day, so you enjoy it, and that's an order!'

And, yes, he did. To my great relief, he didn't even seem to really register that there was only one friend from school there – one who'd now transferred her allegiance to him and followed him around like an adoring puppy – as he was just so excited to see all the things we'd done for him, genuinely thrilled to have been made such a fuss of.

Except at the same time, paradoxically, the atmosphere was just terrible.

'I think I'm going to be mighty glad when this is all over,' Mike commented, when coming into the kitchen to get himself a beer a couple of hours or so into the afternoon.

'Too right, mate,' my brother agreed. And with good reason. We'd only been half an hour into the festivities when it became clear that Justin just had no idea how to behave on such an occasion – his social skills, clearly tested to the limit at the sort of unstructured event that a party for a child this age was, were clearly pretty hopeless. He seemed unable to enjoy his party without spoiling it for the other children, snatching toys, throwing sand, splashing the younger ones way beyond fun. It wouldn't have been so bad if he'd just been over-excited and unable to see it, but it was obvious to everyone that he *could* see he was upsetting them, which only seemed to serve to make him worse. It was now around four and we were all becoming weary – the other children were trying really hard to be patient with Justin, but I could tell it was wearing thin. And once again my little niece was in tears.

'Should I go and have another sterner word with him, d'you think?' I asked Mike. I had already gently chastised him on a number of occasions, but had been reticent about the idea of getting more heated or imposing sanctions because this was not an ordinary situation and this was not an ordinary child. His behaviour – more like that of an overbearing pre-schooler – was like it was for a reason. But it was becoming hard; inside my head I could feel the weight of disapproval of all the other adults, all waiting for me to call a halt to his behaviour and feeling aggrieved that I'd not sufficiently put my foot down.

But Mike shook his head. 'I think leave it,' he said, after considering for a moment. 'Why don't we do the cake, and calm everything down for a bit? Tarika's parents will be coming to collect her in twenty minutes anyway, and after she's gone we can start to wind things down. In the mean-time –' he turned to my brother and grinned – 'another beer's the best way, I think …'

I didn't tackle Justin about his suitcase until the day after the party. The following evening, in fact, when I knew we could have an undisturbed half an hour alone together.

I was out in the conservatory, having a cigarette, while Justin kicked a ball around the garden. He was getting puffed and I could see he was breaking out in a sweat, so I suggested he come and sit with me for a rest.

'You've lost a bit of weight lately,' I commented, as he flopped down beside me. 'All this football must be doing you good. Tell you what,' I added, stubbing out my ciga-rette and turning to face him, 'it won't be long before you're off going to matches with our Kieron.'

'I don't know about that,' he said, grinning, 'but I am getting thinner, aren't I?'

'Yes, you are, love,' I agreed. I paused for a second. 'But you know, you'll also have to cut back on all the sweets and stuff too. If you want to get seriously fit, you will, anyway.'

'I know,' he said, groaning. 'But it's so *hard*. You always have such nice stuff in your cupboards! You'll have to starve me, prob'ly.' He laughed, then. 'Only joking about that, C!'

This, I decided, was a very good moment. He was clearly relaxed and in a jolly sort of mood. *And* we were on the subject of food. Perfect. 'Listen, love,' I said to him then. 'Can I ask you about something? I'm not annoyed –' I put a hand on his arm to reassure him – 'I'm just puzzled. When I was cleaning your room yesterday, I came upon your suitcase, and it was so heavy I couldn't move it ... and, well, I saw all your food ...'

'I didn't steal it!' he said straight away, immediately defensive.

'I wasn't suggesting you did,' I told him gently. 'I just wondered where –'

'I bought it. I bought *all* of it,' he said. 'I get it from the supermarket by the school, with my pocket money. It's my money, isn't it? I can buy what I like with it.'

'I *know* that,' I said soothingly, looking again into his eyes. He was feeling cornered, I could see that, but he wasn't raging, and wasn't about to. Like this, he wasn't a force to be reckoned with at all. He was exactly what he was. A small, upset, bewildered child. It seemed clear to me that even he wasn't sure what had driven him to collect it.

'An' why do you think it's any of your business, anyway?' he persisted, though not at all aggressively.

I shrugged. 'I suppose it's not,' I said. 'As you say, it's your money. But I just wondered – what were you planning on doing with it?'

This seemed to fox him. He looked genuinely confused by the question. And as he thought about it – it was obviously he was trying to find an answer – he also seemed increasingly upset. He shrugged his shoulders, hung his head, then did something completely unexpected. He burst into tears. So I immediately gathered him into my arms.

'Shh …' I said quietly, smoothing his hair, still slightly damp from the football. 'It's okay. It's okay. I just think that maybe if you could explain to me why you have it … if we could talk about it, then …'

'I don't *know* why,' he said, sobbing. 'I just … sometimes just have to eat. I just have to have it there, so I've got it …'

'Just in case.'

I felt him nod. 'It's just like … it's like I've got this big hole in my stomach. An' it makes me feel sick, and it hurts, and it's there all the time, so I eat to try and make it go away.'

'And does it?'

He shook his head now. 'It *never* goes away. No matter how much I eat, it's, like, it just keeps on happening. It doesn't work. I can never fill it up.'

'Like you're empty all the time.'

'Yes, empty. It's like a hole, you know.' He moved his arm to show me. 'Right here. And I just want it to go away. And it never does.'

'But it can,' I said gently. 'But not by eating. You know that. Because it doesn't come from your stomach – not really.' I gently placed my hand back on his head, desperately searching for a suitable analogy, 'It comes from up *here*, Justin. It's because of all the bad things that have happened to you, and all the bad things you remember. But because it's so difficult for your mind to try to think about them, you get that tummy ache – that hole in your stomach you describe. So what we need to do is find a way we can start to make things better. You know what I do?'

He turned to look at me. 'You get those feelings?'

'Of course I do, sweetheart. *Everyone* does, sometimes. And what I do is I try to think of my mind like a big wardrobe, and that all the mixed-up thoughts in my mind are like a pile of messy clothes. A bit like your real messy clothes, when you throw them around your bedroom. And what you need to do with messy clothes is to tidy them all away. So with your thoughts – your messy clothes – you do exactly the same thing. You pick up each one – each horrible thought you have, one by one – then you give it a good shake. Straighten it out, see it in daylight, make sure you've shaken out the creases, and once it's straight enough to be folded, you can fold it and put it back. Tuck it away back in the wardrobe, nice and tidy.'

Justin nodded. 'That seems a funny thing to do,' he said, sniffing.

'Funny, but also good. It works for me every time. I know it's hard to think hard about thoughts you don't like – just like I don't like having to pick up your smelly socks

– and sometimes your mind just wants to forget all about them, but then you end up with that horrible feeling inside. So worth a try, d'you think?'

'Maybe. Yes, okay. I'll try it.'

We made a deal then, sitting side by side in the conservatory. That Justin would keep his stash where it was, for the time being, but that sometimes he'd bring some of the treats downstairs, and we'd share them, the two of us, while we sat and watched the soaps.

Which felt like progress. So, so heartbreaking, but definitely progress. I really hoped we could continue like this.

Chapter 13

'Aw, Mum. Pleeeeaaase!!!'

It was another hot, sunny afternoon on a Wednesday in early June and, listening to my son, you could be forgiven for thinking that he was not a 19-year-old grown man, but a little boy. He really was that plaintive. 'Look at him, Mum,' he was entreating. 'Just *look* at him. How can we *not* keep him? He just looked so sad and so lonely that I couldn't help myself. I really couldn't. Go on, Mum. Say yes. Let me keep him. *Pleeaassee*?'

It could be argued that since I was on something of a mission to rescue waifs and strays myself, I had no business putting up any sort of fight here, but, still – it seemed Kieron had set his sights on the 'strays' a bit rather more literally than I had. For what I saw in front of me, quivering in mild terror in Kieron's arms, was the scruffiest little mongrel I'd seen in a long time.

Not that this unexpected animal visitor should have surprised me; both the kids had been animal mad all their lives and, as a consequence, I'd become a regular Doctor Doolittle. Our house had always been home to a fair few of them at any one time. Most memorable had been a one-eared 'house' rabbit, called Flopsy – so called because she flat-out just refused to be outside, not to mention refusing to use a litter tray either, and insisted on always sleeping with Riley. That relationship, however, was, of necessity, short lived – after a few months, my vacuum cleaner staged a revolt, having become sick of being clogged up by rabbit droppings.

Naturally, to 'ease the pain' of having to let Flopsy go, I was somehow talked into buying a pair of chipmunks, Alvin and Theodore, complete with a seven-foot square cage – erected in the back garden – which housed what looked like a chipmunk-sized assault course. We also had numerous hamsters over the years, who, being hamsters, all died within a couple of years, causing tears and recriminations all round, and even once, when the kids were teenagers, a hamster funeral. Add in a couple of cats, too many goldfish to mention and the odd budgie – *that* was just how animal sick we all were.

But the last straw, two years back, had been our lovely dog Candy. She was a gorgeous Lhasa Apso, and she was stolen from our garden.

Lhasa Apsos are beautiful dogs, very rare and very coveted. And at around £800 for a dog with a good pedigree, it's not surprising that they are coveted by thieves.

But we didn't care about her pedigree, and didn't even really know about it when we got her. She was just a part of our family, and we loved her.

As seemed to be the case now, we'd come upon Candy quite by chance. Kieron had been desperate for us to get a dog – nothing different there, then – so we had agreed to visit our local rescue centre and take a look. We went almost daily for about three weeks in our quest, and pretty soon the staff there knew us all by name, and Kieron used to walk the dogs for them and help feed them. Naturally, he fell in love with each and every one of them, and insisted that any one of these dogs would be the 'perfect' pet. One of the animal carers, however, a young man called Stuart, told Kieron that he would know exactly when he had found the right one because, ultimately, the right dog would choose *him*.

One morning, the rescue centre phoned us to tell us that a new dog was due in. Her owner had been taken ill and was going into a long-term nursing home, and they wondered if we could take Kieron up to meet her. So we did and the two of them became a match made in heaven, Kieron realising, when this lovely sandy little dog immediately leapt up and licked him, that Stuart had been right – she had chosen him. Within a couple of days, she moved in and immediately beguiled all of us completely, so when we lost her, it really broke our hearts. Since then I had sworn I would never have another pet. It was just too painful an idea to contemplate.

But perhaps all that was about to change because it seemed my still animal-mad son had now taken it upon himself to visit the local kennels, and had come home with this equally daft-looking little mongrel.

'Honestly,' I said. 'I can't believe you sometimes! I suppose it'll have to stay with us now, won't it? Be pretty mean to pack him off back there now he's here.'

Kieron had, strategically, I thought, let the dog get down now, and it immediately tried to squeeze itself in between my feet for cover. I bent down and gently stroked his wiry thatch of fur. 'But you should have run it by me,' I pointed out, '*before* going off on your rescue mission.'

'I know, but –'

'And I'm warning you from the outset, I don't do dog poo. Hmm. Or dog walking, for that matter. So it's got to be down to you, okay?'

'I swear, Mum. I promise. You won't have to do a thing. His name's Bob, by the way.'

'Bob? What kind of a name is that for a dog? And I mean it, by the way, about looking after him. I recall "not having to do a thing" for all your previous pets. Very well indeed.'

'I absolutely promise, Mum. I'm older now, aren't I? I'll do everything, I really will. So will Lauren, won't you? She's said she'll take him out for walks when I'm at college.'

Lauren, who had arrived with Kieron but up till now had perhaps wisely kept her counsel (I imagine she thought the sweet-talking was best left to the expert), was another new member of the clan – she was Kieron's new girlfriend. He'd introduced her to us two weeks back, but had in fact been seeing her for about a month before that, after they'd met at a college drama production. Kieron had volunteered to help out with the music and sound effects for the end-of-year show and Lauren, who was a dancer, had spent a lot of time with him.

She seemed to sense that Kieron was different in some way and apparently told him every day who everyone else on the production was and what they did. This was great for him because, Kieron being Kieron, if she hadn't, he'd have simply got on with his job, blissfully unaware of his surroundings, and probably not spoken to anyone else. It can be like that with Aspergers; the way the brain's wired means that boys like Kieron often go into their own little world, seemingly oblivious to what's going on around them. This time, however, thanks to Lauren's emotional intelligence and interest, things were different; he'd made new friends and – really the icing on the cake – had also found himself a lovely girlfriend.

Mike and I were thrilled, as this was the first girl he had ever brought home, and I'd asked him why he'd been so slow to introduce us. Kieron had looked at me as if I was stupid. 'Well, *obviously*, mum,' he'd explained patiently, grinning. 'I wanted to be sure she found me totally irresistible first, so there'd be no backing down when she met the rest of the crew.'

I suppose you really couldn't fault his logic.

Bob, too, became 'one of the crew' very easily, and, true to his word, Kieron did all that I'd asked of him. He and Lauren, from day one, spoilt him as if he were their baby. He slept on a special fleece blanket that Lauren had bought, on the floor in Kieron's room, and they'd buy him treats and toys on what seemed like a daily basis. If they had any money spare, it went on Bob. So no nagging was required – none at all. Another bonus was that Justin took to Bob in a big way, too, always fussing over him, and very quickly it became the norm that wherever Bob was, you'd find Justin, especially when Kieron was in college.

He was a likeable dog, with a really lovely temperament, and, at three years old, didn't come with all the usual puppy hassles of having your house chewed half to death. He was also very obliging, which he needed to be, because Justin never gave him more than five minutes' peace; if he wasn't insisting that Bob sit on his lap, so he could make a fuss of him, he was endlessly feeding him treats or trying to teach him tricks.

There was one big negative aspect to all this, however, which slowly but surely became apparent. It was clear that while Justin was very taken with Bob, he couldn't bear that the rest of us were too. He made it very obvious that he really didn't like it when Bob showed anyone else any affection. If this happened, he would invariably become truculent and irritable, and start saying all sorts of unpleasant things about the dog – often complaining that he'd scratched him, or bitten him. There were definitely shades, I thought, of his history with his mother's dog coming back to haunt him. He just couldn't seem to deal with it if the dog had eyes for anyone but him.

Kieron found this very upsetting. He simply couldn't understand how Justin could say nasty things about an innocent, and also charming, little animal. I tried to reassure him without giving anything away. I knew Kieron would never be able to understand what Justin had done when he was five, however much we might try to explain the extreme nature of the circumstances. With Kieron it was simple: if he had known these sorts of things about Justin's past, he'd find it impossible to be friends with him today. So instead I tried to justify the situation by explaining to Kieron that Justin's mother had had a dog too, and Justin believed that, to her, the dog was more important than her children. Kieron seemed to understand the logic of this so I just suggested he deal with the matter practically – try to keep Bob out of Justin's way a little more, spend time with the dog himself alone, or take him out with Lauren to the park – just the two of them – so that Justin began to learn he couldn't and shouldn't try to monopolise him all the time.

So, yes, I was aware, and, yes, I understood the reasons, but I was still unprepared for what happened next.

It was a Saturday, and Bob had been playing in the garden, while Justin sat in the conservatory, watching him. Kieron and I were in the kitchen with the door open, and from where we were chatting we could see both the garden and the part of the conservatory where Justin was. He had been trying to entice Bob to come to him by bouncing a ball, but the dog was too concerned with chasing birds. And when he did come in – we'd both glanced up when we heard him scampering and skittering across the conservatory floor – it was to see something completely unexpected and so shocking: Justin was punching him in the head.

'What the hell do you think you're doing?' Kieron shouted at him. 'You spiteful little git! What's he ever done to you?' He went straight up to Justin then, towering over him. 'How would you like it if I punched *you* in the face?!' he barked at him. 'Because that's what you deserve!'

I could see this might get ugly, so I rushed to intervene. Kieron looked like he might explode, and I could see Justin – who'd been oblivious to our presence up till now – was really scared of him.

'Love, I'll deal with this,' I told Kieron. 'You just take Bob, okay? Now, Justin,' I began, turning to admonish him. 'That was a very mean thing you did, wasn't it? Poor Bob will be terrified. I want you to go to your room and think about it. You'll be losing points for this, obviously, and –'

But I didn't get a chance to say anything further, because Justin pushed past me and thundered up the stairs to his bedroom, shouting 'Fucking scabby mutt! It bit me! It fucking bit me! But nobody ever listens to me! Oh, no ...'

It wasn't true. We both knew that, because we'd both seen what happened, and Kieron, who was still standing there, holding Bob in his arms, was singularly unimpressed with my scolding. 'You'll be losing points!' he mimicked, with a note of exasperation in his voice. 'Mum, that's not *good* enough! I can't believe that you just said it! How does that *in any way* make up for what he just did?'

In my head I was saying, *you're absolutely right! The punishment really doesn't fit the crime at all!* But what else, I thought miserably, could I do? What would Kieron have me do? Punch him right back in retribution? No, of course not. Unthinkable.

'I know, love,' I said. 'And I'm really, really sorry. Believe me, I'm not going to make this easy for him. He's got to learn, and I'll make sure that he does. I know that won't take away how you feel about it; how could it. But –'

'Too right!' he said, with feeling. His face was a picture of disgust. 'I hate him, Mum. I mean it. Why can't we just send him back?'

I was shocked. I'd never once heard Kieron speak like this. He'd had his moments with Justin, and I was all too aware of those tensions. I'd been so proud of how patient and understanding he'd been. But for Kieron to say he hated Justin was something quite astonishing. My Kieron? My boy who didn't have a bad bone in his body? I'd never heard Kieron say he hated someone, ever. I really felt for him at that moment. I felt awful.

Was this what had happened, I wondered, with all Justin's previous carers? That he'd pushed them to the limit? That, like us, they'd had kids and those kids had demanded that they be released from the constant pressure of having to put up with behaviour, *in their own homes*, which everybody else would find completely unacceptable? Had all those other carers eventually caved in – decided that, ultimately, they had to give their own kids their lives back?

* * *

And that limit would be tested further only a week or so later, when Kieron and I walked into the living room to find Justin, with his back to us, holding Bob in the air by his front legs. To our horror, he was pulling them as wide apart as he could, while the poor dog could do nothing but yelp in agony. It was as shocking a sight as I'd seen in a long time, and I ran towards Justin to stop him. But just as I reached him, he turned and, realising we'd caught him, threw poor Bob, with some force, across the room.

This time it was really too much for Kieron. His eyes full of tears, he picked up his dog and stormed from the room, unable to even look at, much less remonstrate with, Justin. It was horrible, his silence saying so much more than words could; he knew I knew exactly how he felt.

I was sickened and felt desperately sorry for my son, even more so when he announced that same afternoon that Bob was going to go and live at Lauren's for a while. She was going to look after him at her place till such time as he felt it safe for his pet to return. I didn't know what to say to him, much less what to do. I was at a loss to understand Justin's breathtaking cruelty – both to the animal and also to Kieron, who'd done nothing but show him love and understanding from day one. Kieron had already questioned our decision to foster. Now I was seriously questioning it myself.

Chapter 14

'Mrs Watson? It's Richard Firth, Head of Year Seven at the high school. It's about Justin. I'm afraid there's been an incident ...'

Picking up the phone on a weekday was becoming something of a hazardous pastime, I thought ruefully. I couldn't stop the sigh that escaped from my lips, before answering, 'Yes, it's me. What's happened?'

'An incident, as I say, between Justin and another pupil. Quite a serious one this time, I'm afraid.'

'Oh no. What happened?' I asked him again. I was already conscious of a knot forming in my stomach, as if already braced for bad news.

'It happened during a chemistry lesson earlier,' he explained, 'in the science lab,' which sounded rather worrying in itself. 'Another pupil accidently knocked over a beaker of water,' he continued, 'and some of it splashed onto Justin's side of the bench. The teacher concerned has told me that Justin's reaction was completely over the top. He grabbed the girl by the throat, apparently, and pushed her head down against the table, holding a glass beaker over her, screaming for her to apologise –'

'Oh, no.'

'– or he would pour the acid solution in the beaker over her face. And the teacher is pretty sure he intended to, as well. Sad to say, Mrs Watson, but he feels that had he not intervened, Justin would indeed have done just that. The poor girl was hysterical, as you can imagine. So I'm sorry to say that we have no alternative but to exclude him.'

I took a deep breath.

'I understand. So what do you want me to do? Come and get him?'

'If you would, please,' said Mr Firth. 'He's waiting for you now, in the isolation room. If you come into the main reception, someone will take you straight up there. He's rather upset, as you can imagine, now he's calmed down a little. It took two members of staff to remove him from the classroom, I have to tell you. He's a strong boy, and was apparently in quite a rage.

'Anyway, like I said, he's really quite upset now, so if you could come as soon as possible, we'd be grateful.'

'How long is he excluded for?' I asked, already fearing the worst.

'We think it's best if you keep him home now till the beginning of the autumn term,' Mr Firth said. 'He does know this, by the way. And perhaps you could accompany him on his first day back in school? Then perhaps we can all look at strategies that may help him.'

We'd been doing so well, I thought – the incident with Bob notwithstanding – and I'd really felt we were making progress. Indeed, Justin's remorse over what he'd done had seemed so heartfelt and genuine that Kieron had even agreed that Bob could come home, which had been encouraging in itself. Yet here we were again, seemingly back at square one. An overstatement, perhaps, but that's how it felt. One step forward, two steps back. Was this normal?

I also felt a little bit irritable. Unprofessional perhaps, given the job I'd signed up for, but the deal – as was the case with any school-age child – was that on weekdays in term time Justin would be *in* school, leaving me with precious time for the rest of my life, just as happened in any other family.

I was also disappointed with Justin. He had seemed to be making such good progress at school, and had he been able to make it until the end of term, this would have been a real milestone. He had never been able to remain fully in school for more than a couple of weeks up to now, and to do so this time would have provided a real boost to his self-esteem.

But it was not to be. All my plans about deep cleaning the house and spending a few days 'baby shopping' with Riley, who was now very noticeably pregnant, would have to be put on hold. Justin would now be having an extra week at home, and that was that. I was not in the best of moods, therefore, when I arrived at the school to collect him, and I had to confront him with the very serious nature of his actions.

I'd got most of it out of my system on the way home, pointing out how disappointed I was that he'd lost his rag so completely, and also to reflect on exactly what might have happened had the teacher not immediately intervened. How much worse might it have been? I'd also come down hard – I'd felt the time had come to be so – on what was becoming a litany of a typical twelve-year-old's excuses: 'But she said ... but he said ... but, but, but, but ...'

'And you're going to lose points, of course,' I told him, once we'd got home and were continuing the conversation in the kitchen. I tapped the chart on the fridge freezer. 'So I'm sorry to say you won't be able to buy your usual privileges ...' His expression, I could see, was now changing. And not, it appeared, for the better. 'Justin,' I said, exasperated, on seeing it. 'You *know* how these things work, for goodness sake! You've been told enough times! You have to realise that actions have consequences! And you need to think about those consequences *before* you act, not after. And it wouldn't hurt for you to reflect on how much you terrified that poor girl. How do you think *you'd* like it to be pinned down and threatened by someone who was so much bigger and stronger than –'

But I didn't manage to get to the end of my small tirade, because Justin suddenly yanked something out of his jacket, pulling frantically to free it from the edge of the pocket, where it had caught. And I could see from the way he was struggling to pull it out that it was obviously something quite big and hefty. It was only when he lifted it and put it against the side of his head that I realised what it was – it was a staple gun. The sort of staple gun they use in schools to staple posters to walls. A big, heavy staple gun, with a trigger.

'Justin, where did you get that?' I snapped at him, horrified.

'I stole it!' he came back at me, his voice high with anger. 'I stole it from school and there's nothing you can do about it!'

'Put it down, Justin,' I said, trying to keep my voice firm and level. I took a step towards him. 'Come on, hand it over. This is ridiculous. You've been told off because you've done something wrong, and the first thing you want to do is to –'

'Shut up!' he screamed at me. 'Just shut up, okay? One more word out of you and I'll shoot it, I swear!'

'Justin,' I tried again. 'Stop being silly, now. That would hurt you, *really* hurt you, if you pulled that trigger, trust me. Come on,' I said, conscious, even as I did so, that Justin had no fear of hurting himself, did he? So why would that act as any sort of deterrent? Even so, I had to say it. Had to say *something*. 'Come, on,' I repeated. 'Give it to me. Hand it over.'

I took another step towards him and then, unbelievably, before my astonished eyes, he did squeeze the trigger, and shot a staple straight into the side of his head. The noise was sickening.

'Oh my God, Justin!' I cried, as two bright blood spots appeared at his temple. 'Look what you've done! Come on, let me take a look at that, you silly b –'

'Fucking get away!' he hissed. 'Just fucking get away from me, okay? You see what your big mouth does? You just can't keep it shut, can you?'

Then, to my consternation, he calmly pulled the staple from his temple, causing two thick tracks of blood to start oozing down his face.

'Justin, please …'

He lifted the staple gun again, this time waving it towards me. 'Just keep away from me,' he growled. 'Or I swear I'll fucking stab you. And you can blab to Mike and Kieron all you like. I don't care!'

I took a deep breath. I was going to have to disarm him. I had to. I needed – badly needed – for him to know who was boss here. This was what *he* needed. Needed as much as he needed anything. Like an out-of-control toddler, all this child really needed was someone to reel him in, to make him stop.

No child wanted this. No child wanted to wield such frightening power. He was less aggressor than a cornered, injured animal. I knew I had to keep that in mind at all times. And, crucially, to convey that to *him*. 'Look, Justin,' I said firmly. 'I don't know what you think you're doing, but you *will* put down that staple gun, I mean it. I don't care how big and strong you think you are. Trust me, if I have to, I *will* take it from you. And I don't care who you blab to about it, either. Okay?'

I kept my eyes locked on his. He was shocked at what I'd said to him. I could see that. And it made it so obvious that he just wasn't used to being spoken to in this way. You created a monster out of a child and that was what happened, I thought grimly. They behaved so monstrously that everyone became too scared to tackle them, just making their behaviour – their lack of self-control – even worse, and so just perpetuating the problem you'd created.

He blinked at me, twice, though said absolutely nothing. And it was in that instant, that I knew I'd got through to him. A second later, the staple gun was thrust down onto the kitchen worktop with a clatter, and Justin stormed off to his room.

I picked it up – it was so heavy; thank God he hadn't taken it upon himself to throw it at me – then took in a long, slow, deep breath, and exhaled it.

Once again, I was standing in the kitchen shaking.

I left Justin to stew for a few hours. I felt we'd reached a watershed in terms of his response to being punished. That, actually, some good would have come from this incident. That perhaps he now knew it should be him worrying about facing *me*, for a change. I felt he was getting too comfortable in the knowledge that whenever he did something unacceptable, it would work in his favour to storm off for a couple of hours, knowing that I would worry and then go up to make things right.

I tried to ring John Fulshaw, but his mobile was off, so rather than ring Harrison Green, who I really didn't want to speak to, I sent an email to John explaining what had happened and asking if he had any suggestions.

When Justin hadn't come down at his regular tea time, my earlier resolve was starting to weaken and I knew that, once again, I would have to be the pacifier. Mike had arrived home from work and after I updated him on the day's events, he too thought that perhaps I should take Justin some food up. 'But don't make *too* much of a fuss,' he counselled. 'Just give him something to eat and then get straight to the point. He'll know then that you're not playing the usual game.'

It was gone seven in the evening when I finally went up to see him. I'd prepared a mug of hot chocolate and brought a couple of biscuits, and hoped that by now he'd be feeling calm enough for us to talk about what had happened. Not the incident with the staple gun – there was nothing to discuss there – but what had happened in school to provoke such a rage, and how best we could find ways to help him deal with his anger. He was clearly carrying so much distress and hurt that it was an unremitting pressure; threatening to spill over into violence at the slightest thing.

As I knocked softly on the door, I was feeling calmer too. The solution was to talk, and to talk, and to talk. He needed to be listened to. Needed to have his voice heard.

There was no answer, and I wondered if he'd already fallen asleep, so I pushed open the door and went in. The sight that greeted me, however, was in some ways more distressing than the ugly scene in the kitchen that afternoon.

Justin was sitting on his bed, in his pyjamas, his knees bent almost to his chin and his feet bare. In his hands was a shard of CD that he'd obviously broken, and his feet, I saw with horror, were a mess of sticky blood.

He looked up at me, quite calmly, and then followed my gaze, which had come to rest on the full extent of the damage he'd done to himself. He'd gouged holes all around his nails, the skin livid, torn and bloody, and had actually managed to pull both of his big toenails clean off.

I couldn't help it. My eyes filled with tears and as I held out my hand for the jagged bit of plastic, I began crying. He handed it to me passively, without words.

He began climbing into bed then. 'Justin, stop,' I said. 'Wait. I have to clean those …'

He waited. I put the hot chocolate and biscuits on the bedside table, then ran to the bathroom for cotton wool and antiseptic and warm water and plasters, my eyes, all the while, still misted by tears.

When I returned, he sat silently while I attended to his feet, and, feeling far too emotional for words now myself, I was happy for him to be so. We needed to talk, but the time wasn't now.

'Into bed now,' I said, finally, once I was all done. I stood up. 'I'm sure you'll feel better in the morning.'

It felt ridiculous to even think that, let alone voice it, but what else was there to say but a platitude? Of *course* he wouldn't feel any better in the morning because he already felt better right *now*. He felt better because he'd subjected himself to physical agony to still the desperate pain of all the stuff that was clamouring inside his head. He felt better because he'd torn his feet to shreds and pulled off two toenails. What an impossibly high mountain we still had to climb. 'Drink your chocolate,' I said finally. 'Before it gets cold.' Then I stooped and kissed his head, and left the room.

I felt in bits, I realised, as I walked slowly back down stairs. Out of my depth, and in bits.

Chapter 15

After the whole issue of the exclusion and Justin's further bout of self-harming, if you'd asked me what would be the very last thing he needed right now, seeing his mother would have definitely topped the list.

Yet, apparently, that was what was going to happen.

I'd heard nothing from Harrison Green for quite a long time, though I did know John Fulshaw had spoken to him, following my call about the recent school exclusion. And he hadn't been terribly helpful, John confided. When he'd asked about perhaps getting some more support put in place, Harrison's response, according to John, had been bordering on the flippant. A sort of 'Kids, eh? Who'd have 'em!' kind of attitude. It was an attitude that struck me – even if it had been said in jest – as somewhat unprofessional under the circumstances. And John had agreed.

Unsurprisingly, therefore, I wasn't too thrilled to be hearing from Harrison now. And it wasn't just because I

188

had my issues with him personally, either – but because what he was saying to me today completely took my breath away.

'Yes, it's good news,' he announced breezily, having gone through the motions of asking how Justin was doing, yet not appearing at all interested in my answers. 'Janice has told me she's willing to see him.'

Willing? How dare she be '*willing*' to see him! '*Oh*, is she?' I answered, not even trying to keep the sarcasm out of my voice.

He seemed not to hear it – or, if he had, he wasn't playing ball. 'Yes, she feels she's ready to have some contact with him again. She's willing to give him another chance.'

I felt my blood boil. That word again, 'chance'. I was livid. Like she was doing Justin – doing all of us – such a big favour. Like she didn't actually have any responsibility for him at all. It was her and not him who should be all out of chances. 'Oh, is that right?' I answered shortly. 'How very gracious of her. And when is this "contact" meant to happen?'

'This Friday,' he said brightly. 'If it's not too much trouble for you both.'

Stupid man, I thought. Of course it would be trouble. Had he completely forgotten that Mike had a full-time job and that Janice lived several hours' drive away? Did he really think it was that simple for him to take a day off work? At three days' notice?

God, how I hated his tone. He seemed so totally focussed on keeping this woman sweet, and to hell with the damage it might do to Justin. I wasn't stupid. I knew that in almost all cases promoting and keeping contact with a child's birth family was crucial to their sense of identity. I also knew, and understood, that, again, in most cases, a child could see no wrong in their parents, and craved their love and affection, however paltry the amount they received. But was it just me who saw right through Janice? Was it just me who saw how manipulative she was? How she got everyone around her dancing to her tune? Including Justin. And including Harrison Green.

'No trouble at all,' I said sweetly, not wanting to give him any reason to think I was going out of my way to be obstructive. He wanted Friday, he'd bloody get Friday. 'What is it this time?' I added, my voice, by itself, growing even more sugary. 'New bloke on the scene, is it? New boyfriend to try and impress? Or just some more bad news for Justin that she's anxious to pass on?' I knew I was being childish; it wasn't Harrison Green who was the monster here. But I wondered, and not for the first time these past months, if he knew anything like as much about Justin as I now did. Had he bothered to read up on all the new things John Fulshaw had found out for me? I didn't think so. Not for a minute.

'I've no idea, Casey,' he answered, sounding just a tiny bit irritable now. 'She just rang me and asked if she could see him this week. She probably feels bad about what happened last time. Wants to put things right. Try again.'

I nearly choked on the bile that rose in my throat as he said this. Did he *really* believe that? If so, he was even more naive than I'd thought. 'Okay,' I said, 'as long as Mike can arrange a day off work, we'll take him up there for a few hours on Friday. Only this time, I think we'll stick around.'

Justin himself was as happy as Larry when I told him. He was like the cat with the cream; simply couldn't stop beaming. It was as if he'd completely forgotten what had happened the last time; not at all that he remembered and was just putting on a brave face. Quite the contrary. It was as if it had never happened at all.

It was now early August – a whole seven months since Justin had last seen his mother. Their only contact in the interim had been via the continuing strained (and now rather sporadic) phone call he was allowed to make to her, still always heartbreaking in its awkwardness and banality.

It was heartbreaking *not* to listen. Justin was allowed to call his mother weekly – and she was encouraged to phone him often, although that barely happened (and only at times when I knew she'd had a recent visit from social services). Of course, whenever I reminded Justin that it was phone time, he would often make excuses not to ring. 'Oh, she'll be bathing the kids at this time,' he'd say. 'I'll ring another day. I promise'

Recognising his reluctance – and why wouldn't he be reluctant, given how toe-curling their 'conversations' were to overhear? I'm sure I would be – I never pushed it, but just let him phone her whenever he asked.

Which wasn't often. Thinking about it, I now realised that I couldn't actually recall when last they'd spoken. She would now, I also realised, be quite heavily pregnant, if not actually due. I hoped her hormones didn't add to what would be a stressful encounter, by making her any more volatile that she'd already proved to be.

It was a sultry sort of day, the kind you often see in August, and not the best kind of conditions in which to embark on a long drive. Though the oppressiveness of the atmosphere, as we sped along the motorway, was, at least, a match for my own heavy heart. I'd had a bad feeling about this visit from the off, and it was stubbornly refusing to go away.

We arrived at the house at around eleven in the morning. 'Lovely day for it,' observed Mike cheerfully, as Justin gathered up his stuff. He'd brought his portable Nintendo so he could play games on the journey, and his favourite hoodie, which he now shrugged back on. Beneath it he wore a T-shirt with a wrestling image on it. It was one his mum had bought him – a couple of years ago, by the look of it – and was really much too small for him. I'd tried to talk him out of it, joking that his mum would think we hadn't bought him any clothes, but he was adamant. So I let him have his way.

I looked out of the car window at the run-down estate, taking in the overgrown gardens with chunks of fencing missing, and the stray detritus of broken furniture and abandoned, buckled toys. I felt anything but cheerful, but I kept up a facade of jollity and smiles, for Justin's sake. I could see just how nervous he was about seeing her – this woman who'd caused him so many years of pain.

They must have been looking out for us, because the front door opened within seconds of us pulling up outside, though the first glimpse I got of Janice was very fleeting. She stood in the doorway, her hand shielding her eyes from the sun as she squinted across the garden to get a look at me. As I got out, to let Justin out, I smiled in her direction, politely raising my hand in a little wave. She smiled back but immediately turned around and walked back inside leaving the front door open ready, but unmanned, for Justin.

Some welcome, I decided, as Justin clambered from the back seat. I'd have at least expected that she would come out and greet us, however briefly. But then, I thought, given all that had happened since we'd had him, perhaps we were the 'enemy'. There was no logic to that, obviously, but I felt it even so. Could she feel the ripples of my disapproval swirling like a noxious mist down her front path?

'I've got my mobile,' I whispered, as I gave Justin a quick kiss and hug goodbye. 'We'll just be in town, so ... well. You know ... when you're ready for us to come back and get you ...'

He nodded once, his eyes bright, and trotted meekly down the path. Watching him go, I felt he suddenly looked so young.

We got back into the car just as the front door closed behind him.

'Ding ding, round two,' Mike said, softening his words with a grin. 'So, while they're at it, love, where shall we go, then?' I grinned too, but it didn't matter how much we tried to make light of it; we were both braced, like coiled springs, for the next meltdown.

Shopping. That was the best thing. Take my mind off it all. 'Driver,' I said, in my best upper-class voice, 'to a baby shop, please. And make it snappy!'

The call came from Justin about an hour and a half later. We'd been mooching round the shops, our minds not really on booties and buggies and baby paraphernalia, but on him, and I heard my phone straight away because I'd been walking around with it in my jacket pocket. I'd popped it in there because I never heard it in my handbag – voicemail always beat me to it – and this was one call I didn't want to miss.

But even so, it was a call no normal caring person would have wanted to take either. Justin was crying, crying hard, really howling down the phone.

'Come and get me, Casey, please,' he sobbed, amid all sorts of other noise. It sounded like there was some sort of struggle going on. And I could hear his mother shouting at him as clearly as I could hear him. So she must, I thought, really be giving it some welly. And she was. 'Yeah, that's right, grass, you just do what you do best! Fucking little grass, you are – as if I don't have enough on my fucking plate! Go on then –' there were more sounds, all too difficult to identify. 'Go on, hit me if you think you're fucking hard enough!'

Her voice cut through the other sounds like fingers down a blackboard. I wondered briefly what the two little ones must be thinking about all this. What a thing to witness. It was shocking.

I started shouting too, then, in order to be heard.' Justin! *Justin*!' I said. 'It's okay, love. Keep calm. We're just in town, okay. We'll be there in five or ten minutes, no more. Just try to keep calm. We're on our way.'

'Okay,' I heard him say. 'But hurry, Casey, please! She's a psycho! She's punching me …'

Once again, Janice's voice cut through his sobbing, even as I kept trying to reassure him. By now, the two of us were jogging back through the shopping mall to the exit. 'You're the fucking nut-job!' she screeched at him. 'Making all that shit up to the social workers! Spit at me again an' I swear I'll knock you out, you little bastard! *No* fucker wants you, you hear? So they'd better fucking hurry …'

I only hung up once we reached the underground car park. My hand was shaking violently. Five or ten minutes. Could we honestly get there in five or ten minutes? And, anyway, what might have happened by then? I filled Mike in on what I'd heard Janice say, fighting to keep my voice level as he pulled out into the beginnings of the early rush-hour traffic and we sped off. His face was white with anger, and he was driving far too fast. 'Calm down,' I kept saying. 'Watch your speed. Watch your speed, Mike!'

'Why?' he spat. But I knew he wasn't talking about his speed. 'Why do we have to do this, eh, Case? Why are we being made to keep putting this kid *through* this? *Eh*? God, isn't he already damaged enough?'

When we reached the house I could see Justin peering out of a front window. He disappeared from view almost as soon as I saw him, and reappeared soon after, running out of the front door. He came straight up the path and started tugging at the passenger door even before I'd had a chance to unlock it for him. I clambered out, and immediately saw his dirty, tear-stained face. He was clearly desperate to be gone so I flipped the back of my seat down and helped him into the back, aware, as I looked back, that Janice was once again in her doorway, but now she wasn't smiling. She was shouting, really loudly.

'Go on, fuck off!' she railed at us all, waving her hand in wide arcs. 'Go on, fuck off the lot of you, you fucking snobs! Poking your fucking noses in my business! How dare you! It's all your fucking fault, is all this!'

She was pointing straight at me as she said this and I found myself wavering. Between getting back into the car and marching up to her to give her a piece of my mind. She might think she was scary but she didn't frighten me.

But Mike, I suspect, must have noticed my body language. 'Casey!' he snapped. 'Just get in the car. Now!'

Fuming, I jumped in and clamped my lips tight together. He was right. A ranting tirade from me would help nothing. Would probably make things even worse. It was probably the last thing Justin needed to witness. He'd suffered more than enough adults who preferred to behave like children, and there was no way on earth that I wanted to join their sorry ranks. It was hard though. Hard to leave her there shouting the odds, unchallenged. This was so wrong. It took many, many miles for me to calm down.

Justin was silent, completely silent, all the way home. We didn't press him. He'd talk when he felt able to talk. Best for now that we didn't attempt to process what had happened. Best thing would be for him to sleep. Which he did.

It felt like a very long journey back. No-one spoke, Justin because he'd clearly withdrawn into himself, and me because I didn't dare open my mouth; I was too terrified of what would come out of it. Mike just drove, his eyes resolutely fixed on the road ahead. The time for post-mortems would be later.

Once in the house, Justin went straight up to his bedroom, refusing all offers of something to eat or drink.

'That's fine, love,' I reassured him, plonking my bag down and stretching. I felt stiff and drained, both inside and out. 'No wonder you're not hungry,' I added, squeezing his shoulder. 'You can have something later. I've got crumpets in ...'

But he didn't want to know. He was too locked into his misery to even acknowledge me properly. He was off up the stairs, barely registering my words.

'Let him be, love,' Mike counselled. 'Come on, let's get ourselves a drink, eh?' He shook his head. 'What a day, eh? What a day.'

And a day, it turned out, that wasn't yet over.

Barely a minute had passed – I was still boiling the kettle – when we became aware of a racket going on above our heads. We exchanged a look, and moved as one out of the kitchen and up the stairs, Mike, ahead of me, taking the treads three at a time.

'He's barricaded the door,' he said, trying and failing to enter Justin's bedroom. The sounds, this close up, were much more obvious, as well as louder. He was smashing things up. Precisely what, we didn't know. But there was stuff being thrown, being broken, being stamped on. And we couldn't get in to calm him down.

'Oh, God,' I said. 'Justin! *Justin!*'

Mike put a hand on my arm. 'Let's give it a second or two,' he whispered, with his usual calm wisdom. 'Let him get it out of his system. It's only things, after all. Stuff. All replaceable. Let's just give him a moment and let him get it out.'

I reflected miserably that maybe the next thing we bought him should be a punchbag. But, sure enough, within a minute, the noise completely ceased. But it was the briefest of respites, for less than another thirty seconds later. It was replaced by another, even more sickening sound.

It was immediately obviously what it was. 'He's banging his head against the wall, Mike,' I whispered. Mike nodded. His face set in a grimace. 'So now we *must* go in,' he said. 'Stand back a moment, love.' Upon which he promptly shoulder barged the door.

Mike's a big guy, and the door didn't offer much resistance, the pile of stuff Justin had wedged against it tumbling away.

Justin himself seemed oblivious to us. He was crouched in the corner, and, as we'd guessed, was banging his head, really thumping it against the wall. Mike strode across the room and sat straight down beside him, but Justin immediately turned, his face streaked with dirty tears, and started pummelling Mike instead, going for it, really punching him.

Mike took a few blows, all the time trying to soothe him, whispering, 'Okay, lad, it's okay. Shhh. I know … it's okay …' but eventually he had to use his size and strength as well, pulling Justin close into him and pinning his arms, till the rage inside him began to lose intensity.

I could hardly bear watch – my own rage was too great. I had to leave this one to Mike, and go downstairs. I needed to calm *myself* down if I was going to be of any use.

How could *any* mother, however feckless, hurt her baby so?

Chapter 16

I woke up the next morning with a really thick head – not because I'd spent the night before drowning my sorrows, but because I'd hardly been able to sleep a wink. Funny, I thought ruefully, snuggling up against Mike's comfortable bulk – boy, was I glad it was Saturday – I'd never really thought about sleep deprivation in all this. That was for foster parents who looked after little babies, wasn't it? Not strapping twelve-year-old boys.

I closed my eyes and tried hard to let sleep reclaim me for a bit – I had no plans for the day, bar, perhaps, catching up with Riley; though I saw plenty of her I was acutely aware that, in my head, at least, Justin seemed to be taking all my attention, when what I really craved was enough space and mental energy to enjoy the latter stages of my little girl's first pregnancy; I wanted to be there for her, support her, not be so preoccupied and worried all the time.

Which brought me back, full circle, to the events of the previous day. How could a mother treat her own child with such breathtaking cruelty? It didn't seem to matter how much I or anyone made excuses, it simply went against every maternal instinct in the world for Janice to behave as she had done.

I wasn't naive. Wishing for some whimsical utopia was just silly. The fact was that this woman was unable, for whatever reason, to give her child a single iota of love. She obviously saw him as an adversary now as well; her words to him yesterday, screamed out as we were leaving, made it clear that there were only two reasons she'd asked to make contact: one was as a sop to social services about the adequacy of her 'mothering' and the other – entirely related to the first one – was to make it clear to him that potentially he'd made things precarious for her, by prompting them to investigate her and her other children further.

But my anxieties went deeper than my fury at Janice. I couldn't help wondering what good we were doing. Whether, in the last stressful eight months of his life, we'd actually helped Justin much at all. Sure we'd given him a home and security and boundaries. And we'd certainly given him a healthy amount of good old-fashioned love. But I was full of self-doubt. Really – were we actually helping him? Was anything we did going to help him in the long run to become someone able to find peace within himself and in the world?

Or was it (as, in my exhausted state, seemed to be more the case) that in reality we were conducting not much more than a holding exercise? Providing a roof over his head, and little more? It certainly felt that way to me at the moment. That we were unearthing a whole Pandora's box full of issues, none of which I felt we had the power to help resolve.

'Absolute nonsense! Not true!' said John Fulshaw, with feeling, when I finally got hold of him a couple of hours later. I smiled at that; he was echoing what Mike had remarked earlier, when, whey-faced and gloomy, I'd taken him up a cup of tea. I'd also looked in on Justin, who'd been sleeping like a baby. He'd looked exhausted, and would probably sleep till noon, if we let him. Just looking down at his sleeping form made my blood really boil. For all that had happened, I knew he would forgive his mother *anything*, if she would just make some small gesture towards allowing him to believe that somewhere deep down she loved him and wanted him.

'I really appreciate your confidence,' I told John now, having run through the sickening events of the previous day and evening. 'But that's really not how it feels to me. But the main thing is Janice. I feel really strongly about this, John. Seeing her is not helping him at all. It really isn't. Whatever she tells Harrison Green, I have seen the results. And trust me, if he had, he'd desist from this whole idea that the contact, in the current situation, is useful. Trust me, if he'd been there watching Justin banging his head against the wall last night, he'd think twice. The only reason she really had Justin there was to warn him off and punish him, whatever soft-soaping clap-trap she told social services. Honestly, John, if you saw her you'd see what I mean. It was like she was a twelve-year-old herself – not a mother. Just some hysterical pubescent girl ranting at him. All visiting her is doing is reinforcing his feelings of being a bad person, unloved because he's unlovable, full stop. Can you imagine what it's like to be constantly told by your own mother that you're evil and that nobody wants you? I'd have thought he'd already learned that message enough. Twenty times too many, in fact.'

John sighed. 'I'm so sorry, Casey. It's not right to put you and Mike through all this either. We're going to have to rethink the whole contact situation, aren't we? That blasted woman just can't keep on doing this.'

I smiled wryly to myself again at his polite choice of words for Janice. I could think of lots of them, right now, and, non-PC though it might be, the word 'blasted' didn't feature on my list.

'Tell you what I'm going to do,' he said. 'I'm going to call Harrison Green right now and suggest – no, insist – that our own team's birth-family therapist gets involved with the case.'

'And you'll suspend contact for the time being?'

'Yes, I think that's the way forward, depressing an option though that is, for all concerned. But the right decision, I think. Linda – that's her – can go and do some home visits with her. Make a thorough assessment, maybe even insist Janice goes to parenting classes –'

'She'd do that, you think?'

'She's not really in a position to argue, is she? So let's let Linda assess things and then give us feedback on what she feels is the best way forward. That work for you?'

'Yes, it does. It's definitely better that way, I think. Though, of course, Justin will want to see his mother again eventually – not right now, perhaps; he's much too angry with her, obviously – but how do we play it if and when he starts asking if he can?'

'We tell him straight,' said John. 'She's lied to him enough. So we won't. We'll just have to make it clear that she's got some emotional issues that we feel are best sorted before they have contact again. But let's cross that bridge when we come to it.'

'Agreed. And if it becomes an issue, I guess we can rethink as and when. But ...'

'Yup?'

'In the meantime, I think we need more support here. I know you're pushed, but I've been thinking lots about it lately, and I feel the lines just keep blurring too much. We're supposed to be *in loco parentis*, Mike and I, but I feel I'm increasingly playing the role of counsellor with him, which makes it difficult for all of us to provide a stable, relaxed home. It's one thing him and I having our chats over hot chocolate – that's good and normal and reassuring for him, obviously – but once I'm trying to 'counsel' him I feel it's in danger of becoming counter-productive. It's not right for him to start coming home feeling he might be due a 'therapy session before tea' – you know? – whether he feels like it or not. Home should feel a place where he doesn't have those pressures, shouldn't it?'

It was funny; we'd learned all about this in training, all the different roles various professionals needed to play in the life of a child stuck in the care system. It had felt complex – most of it like gobbledegook, really, and Mike and I had often raised our eyebrows at all the jargon that was contained in the many handouts we got given to take home.

But, suddenly, once you're doing it in real life, all that changes. You start dealing with real children, and it starts making sense. So we just sort of picked it up, along the way, as we went. Fostering is many things, but it's never, ever boring. It's always a work in progress, there's always something new to learn.

'Absolutely, Casey,' John agreed now. 'You're spot on. And I've been thinking about that anyway, as it happens, in preparation for him going back to school next month. We have an excellent anger-management counsellor on the programme – name of Simon Cole – and I was thinking that, if we – well, ahem, *you*, I guess! – could persuade Justin to go for it, that we might fix up some sessions with him. Does that sound okay?' It sounded to me more like the title of that American film, with Jack Nicholson and Adam Sandler, but if John thought it would work, I was that last person who'd disagree. 'And look,' he added, 'I know I've said it already, but it really bears repeating. You and Mike are doing a *fantastic* job, you really are. I know it's difficult for you to see yourselves, because you're with him

24/7, but all of us have noticed massive changes in Justin. I'm not just saying that, either. We all have. You know, you should feel really proud of the way you've been handling all these challenges. You were born to do this, both of you, and we feel really lucky to have you on the programme.'

'Okay, okay, enough!' I felt compelled to say, blushing. 'And thanks. It doesn't feel that way to me right at this moment, but I really do appreciate what you're saying.'

'As you *should*,' John replied. 'As I keep saying, and will keep saying –'

But I had to call a halt to all the praises he was singing, reassuring though they were. I could hear Justin coming out of his bedroom. Time to end the call and go and create some of that all-important 'normality'. If there was nothing else I could do, at least I could do that.

'Bacon and egg sarnie, love?' I called up the stairs, brightly. He was hurting a great deal and Mike and I were both worried about further attempts at self-harming; we had been all night and had checked on him constantly.

Pecker up, Casey, I told myself firmly. It was likely to be a long weekend.

The more I thought about the anger-management idea, the better I liked it. I knew it was more about addressing the symptoms than the root of the problem, but, as one of the tools in our armoury, it felt like a positive one. Of course it would be hard for Justin to come to terms with all the terrible things that had destroyed his self-worth and self-esteem – perhaps many, many years of support and regular therapy

– but while there was nothing much anyone could do about his mother's rejection, learning to control his emotions in the here and now was a wholly positive thing to do. It would benefit his self-esteem enormously if he could learn to take better control of himself and so stop having even more opprobrium heaped on his young head, such as had happened at school during the last week of the summer term.

Despite my positive feelings, however, it was exactly the long – and tough – old weekend I'd predicted. We both felt we were only just keeping Justin together. That he was teetering on the brink of complete abject despair. He looked, almost physically, like a scared, wounded animal, who wanted nothing more than to run away from the world for all time; to go to sleep and never wake up again.

Riley came over later that day, anxious, as was ever her caring way, bless her, to hear how the second visit to his mother had gone. When I told her, she was horrified, almost speechless with shock.

'God, how *could* she?' she said, her hand moving in big, gentle arcs over her swollen tummy. I wasn't even sure it was a conscious thing she did, but to me it spoke volumes, as it echoed my own feelings. We were both mothers now, I realised, and the feeling was universal. To see another mother going against that most fundamental of instincts was stunning her just as much as it had me.

'I'd like to kill her,' she decided. 'Well, not *kill* her, Mum, obviously. But for two pins I'd be up there giving her a piece of my mind about exactly what she's doing to her own child. That poor kid. Makes you wonder how he gets through each day. It really does. Poor, poor Justin.'

But it was to be a couple more days before Justin himself wanted to talk about what had happened with his mother.

It was a midweek afternoon and we were sitting together on the sofa, watching some silly slapstick movie. I had loads of chores to do, but I knew better than to do them. The dust and mess could wait for once, even for a stickler like me. He might not want to talk but he needed to know I was close to him.

Justin loved those kinds of movies in particular and would normally sit beside me laughing hysterically and fairly constantly. But today he was quiet and still.

'You okay, babes?' I asked him.

'I'm alright,' he replied. 'I was just thinking about this Simon bloke. What'll happen?'

We'd fixed up the first of Justin's anger-management sessions a couple of days before. Simon was due to be collecting him in the morning, and though, when I'd explained about it, he'd seemed quite receptive, it must obviously have been playing on his mind.

Must be difficult, I thought, to be just twelve years old, and to have complete strangers sit and ask you personal questions all the time. I thought back to Kieron when he was a young boy. He'd go scarlet if a stranger said *anything* to him, even something as innocuous as 'Good morning'.

'Oh, I don't think it's anything to worry about,' I reassured Justin now. 'I don't think you'll have to do anything complicated. He'll probably just want to start to get to know you.'

'Yeah, but *why*?' He had obviously been thinking things through. 'I don't see how he can help me. What can he do?'

I shrugged. 'I'm not sure,' I said truthfully. 'I don't know that much about it. But it could be really useful, you chatting to him about stuff. You just don't know unless you try, do you? I think it's all about trying to look at which things make you angry, and then finding ways to deal with the anger when it comes. You know, like when people get cross about something and say they are going to count to ten instead of shouting. You heard of that?'

He nodded. 'Yeah.'

'So it's sort of like that. Like counting to ten only in more detail. Better than shouting and ranting …'

'I suppose …'

'And better,' I said, '*much* better than hurting your*self*. People do that too, don't they? Like you did on Friday. You get mad and then end up doing damage to yourself. Which is no good, now, is it?'

Justin shook his head. 'No.' Then he turned round to face me, the film now forgotten. 'She's chosen a name for this new kid, you know. It's gonna be called Princess.' He pulled a disgusted face. 'How stupid is that, Casey? What idiot would call a kid Princess?'

'Oh dear,' I said, pulling a bit of a face myself, in solidarity. 'Mind you, look at pop stars. Some of them have *really* daft names for their kids.'

He harrumphed. 'An' you know why she's calling it that? Because she's going to be treated just like a princess, she told me. And have everything she wants, and all that. She was being really mean about my brothers, an' all, too, saying they were ending up like me and how she wished they were never born.'

'That's awful, love,' I said. 'She shouldn't say things like that. No wonder you got mad ...'

'I told her, though,' he said, his voice suddenly animated. 'I told her and I spat at her, because she's wicked. She's a bitch, Casey, and I'm never going to speak to her again. Let her and her spoiled brat princess just carry on. I don't care. I'm not bothered any more.'

He slumped back in his seat and returned his attention to the movie, obviously having said all he needed to about it.

In contrast, I could feel my own anger bubbling up again, fighting to keep my voice even as I tried to console him by saying the very thing that was professional and proper in the circumstances, but at the same time I went against everything I felt.

'Give it time, babes, 'I said softly, 'after all, she is your mum. She was probably just lashing out at you *because* she's pregnant. When you're pregnant, you know, your hormones go all over the place. You know about hormones?' He nodded. 'And you know what we've been saying about Riley, and being all loopy? It does happen. So give it time. Your mum wouldn't have meant it. Not really.'

I could have cried when I saw the flicker of hope in his young eyes.

I felt awful. Felt like a traitor.

Chapter 17

It was late August and, now that Justin was making such great progress with his new counsellor, we decided we could take the plunge and plan a short family holiday. Heaven knew, we all felt that we needed one.

For all my anxieties about Justin's progress having been so patchy, it seemed the anger-management sessions were doing a great deal of good. Simon Cole himself certainly thought so. He told us he was making great strides in getting Justin to understand his anger – where it came from, both in terms of its history and what triggered it, and also in making him realise that his anger towards his mother was something he'd turned, over the years of his short, distressing life, into a generalised anger against *all* women.

Justin was also now keeping a journal, and writing in it regularly, setting down what he was getting from each session. He'd also show this to me and want to talk about the sessions, which was good news all round. Solid progress.

We decided on Magaluf, in Mallorca, because we hadn't been there before, and managed to bag ourselves a last-minute bargain. This was going to be quite a big adventure for Justin, as holidays were a luxury he didn't generally enjoy. He'd only once been abroad, during a previous foster placement, when the couple had taken him to a villa they owned in Greece, which had been okay, he explained to me, but had got a bit boring after a while. It was situated in the middle of nowhere, up a mountain, apparently, and there was absolutely no-one else around. So, left to his own devices much of the time, while they sat and read (improving books, I didn't doubt), he'd struggled to find things to do.

I rolled my eyes, wondering at the wisdom of taking a child like Justin into the middle of nowhere, with no telly, no entertainment and no distractions. Still, foster carers came in all sorts of guises, I supposed, so I shouldn't and wouldn't judge them, and I didn't doubt that, for another child, it would have been perfect, just as a busy corner of sunny Spain would be perfect for this one. Come to think of it, I didn't doubt – and here I smiled to myself – that for a different kind of child joining our extended family and our madhouse might be every bit as much of a challenge. 'Well, brace yourself,' I said, grinning, as I showed him some pictures and reviews on the internet. 'Because this holiday will be nothing like that one. We're staying in a big holiday complex, on a beach, on the edge of a big resort, and there are lots of swimming pools and slides and entertainment and shops and restaurants … So one thing I *can* promise is that you definitely won't be bored!'

I'd already thought of that, in any case, since Justin still found it hard to make friends – I'd asked my sister if we could also take along my niece and nephew, Chloe and Daniel, who were now 13 and 12 respectively. By now they knew Justin well, and they were all rubbing along fine in the main, so I thought it would be a shrewd move to have them there too.

Naturally, everyone was quite happy with this arrangement; my niece and nephew got an extra holiday, my sister and brother-in-law got an unexpected and unscheduled week off, and Riley, who at 29 weeks was now almost too pregnant to travel, knew she would only be on standby for Auntie Riley-type duties, and could make the most of one of her last weeks of peace, quiet and sleep in the balmy surroundings of the sunny Balearics, mostly from the comfort of a big sunbed.

David, unfortunately, couldn't come, because he'd just won a big work contract, and was keen anyway to cram in as many hours now as possible, so he had time and money in hand for those all important, and precious, first weeks after the birth. The only other person who wasn't going to come with us was Kieron. Kieron, being the way he was, really didn't like going on holiday, which in itself was proof positive that parenting is something you really do learn on the job, as it was something we'd only discovered recently.

He'd always come on holiday with us when he was grow-ing up, of course, and his quietness when away we'd put down to the fact that he was a quiet boy in a very noisy family. But a year or so back he'd admitted that holidays, generally speaking, were all a bit much for him. He found it difficult to deal with the change in both his surroundings and his routine. So he was more than happy to stay home, look after Bob, and have his grandparents for company. They'd come to stay and help him house sit while the rest of us were away.

And in what seemed like just a handful of days, we all were.

'It's amazing!' Justin said, as we clambered down off the coach at the complex. He'd been in a state of excitement ever since we'd left the house back in England, and sat glued to the window for the duration of the flight, commenting in awed tones about everything he could see. He was like a shaken bottle of pop, about to blow at any moment. After the long drag of travelling, Mike and I were both glad our timings were such that there'd still be time for the kids to go in the pool for a bit of a splash about. It was very hot, and they all really needed to cool down while we got settled in and had a drink.

But the cooling down, it seemed, didn't actually have the desired effect. Not in Justin's case it didn't, for sure.

We'd decided on Chinese for our first meal of the holi-day. There was a big place only a short walk from the hotel complex, that we'd seen on our way in and which a poster in our hotel's lobby had recommended. It was also good value, being an all-you-can-eat buffet: the ideal place to take three hungry kids.

Right away though, it was clear – both Mike and I noticed it – that Justin was out of his comfort zone. Thinking about it later, I suppose it was something we should have planned for, but it had been a while now since there had been any food issues at home, because Justin had adjusted to our routine. Well, actually, it was more a case of us adjusting to Justin's routine, in that routine mealtimes had now become the norm for us. I'd even convinced myself, I think, that the regime of set mealtimes, with menus planned in advance, was the better option as it took away the stress of having to constantly think what to cook. We did take him to restaurants, but we were organised about that too – always telling him in advance and sticking to the usual schedule.

I'd still made a point of explaining how things would be on holiday, that we'd be eating out a lot and that the timings might vary, but at the same time I reassured him that, whatever the changes, he'd still have three meals and a snack every day.

Justin had seemed to take all this on board, and assured me that he would be fine. Straight away, however, he gave us cause for concern, and I immediately wondered if we'd been over-confident; it was one thing to accept something as a concept in the future, but quite another to have to deal with the reality.

The food was laid out, buffet-style, on a big communal serving area, and, once given his plate and told to help himself, Justin wellied in and did just that. While the rest of us just picked the usual modest quantity of items – knowing, of course, that we could come back for more if we were still hungry – Justin was filling his own plate as if his very survival depended upon it. I was pretty sure he didn't even know what half the items were, but he was piling them on nevertheless, in an ever increasing, and somewhat teetering tower, till bits of food were actually hanging off the rim of his plate.

'What's he *doing*?' asked my niece Chloe, incredulously, as we sat back down at the table. Mike had lingered at the buffet, waiting for Justin to finish choosing, but I could tell that he'd decided not to tackle him about it. I could see him gesturing to him to finish loading up and come back.

My nephew, now alerted to the Desperate Dan-sized meal Justin was now heading back with, giggled as he watched bits fall from the plate as he walked, and the fronds of dangling noodle swinging as he walked.

'Shh, Daniel,' said Riley, who was, like me, clearly clocking a potential scene building as she saw the determined and slightly strange expression on Justin's face. 'You just concentrate on not getting soya sauce down your T-shirt, okay?'

Justin was back then, and once seated, started tucking into his huge plateful. Which, to all our astonishment, he very quickly polished off. Then, before I could even so much as open my mouth to speak to him, he pushed his chair back and headed off to the buffet again.

Once again, Mike and I exchanged nervous glances. What had possessed me to come to a place like this? I thought. This was like a red rag to a bull. All that food, all that choice, all those issues he was struggling with. How could he not feel this compulsion to cram in as much as he could?

He returned with a second plate, just as overflowing as the first one, and began immediately tucking into that one as well. By now I was feeling nauseous just watching him! He was a good half-way through before he floundered and slowed down, but the look of complete focus had not left his face.

'Getting full, mate?' Mike asked lightly, though in truth we were all feeling tense now. I was already aware of a couple of people whispering and nudging each other as Justin had walked by with the second plate, not least because several bits had dropped on the carpet and a waitress had rushed across to gather them up.

'No,' he said shortly, speaking through a mouth full of noodles.

'Come on, love,' I said. 'Don't be silly now. You can't possibly still be hungry.'

'Yes, I am,' he replied defiantly. 'An' it says "All You Can Eat", doesn't it? So that's what I'm going to do.'

His voice had become loud enough so that heads had begun turning. 'I know it does, love,' I tried again. 'But that doesn't mean you have to eat enough for three people. At least try and leave room for some dessert!'

Chloe and Daniel were both cringing by now, their giggles at the spectacle of Justin's super-sized food mountain being replaced by those of embarrassment, as, glowering, he doggedly kept shovelling in food. He was looking ill by now, his face pale and shiny with perspiration, but he seemed determined to cram in every last mouthful. And it seemed he had every intention of finding room for dessert, too, because he now stood up again, with the rest of us still eating, and made a beeline for the trolley at the end of the buffet table, which was piled with a selection of child-friendly things.

This time, however, he didn't even get himself a plate to fill up. He just stood there, to both our and other diners' consternation, grabbing items of fruit, carton jellies and pots of crème fraiche and yoghurt, and cramming as many as he could into his pockets, while stuffing cream cakes in his mouth with his free hand.

Mike was up on his feet and over there just as the staff had started looking anxious; being typically Chinese, they were too polite to say anything outright. But Mike did.

'That's enough,' he said. 'Now put some of that stuff back, please, there's a good lad. You've taken far too much food for one person to eat.'

Justin's reaction was as loud as it was shocking. 'Leave me alone!' he said. 'Just fuck off and leave me alone!' At which point Mike had to take him by the arm and frog-march him back to the table, to a whispered chorus of 'tut!'s and 'ooh er!'s. 'I think it's time,' he said tightly, as they got back to the table, 'for us to pay up for what we've had and call it a night.'

To my immense relief, it seemed Justin had had his fill of Mike's very evident disapproval, and as I hurried over to settle up and apologise to the waitress, Justin headed back out into the street with Mike meekly enough, while Riley, Chloe and Daniel could only look on, aghast.

Once we were back at the hotel, Justin's flash of temper had died down, and he looked contrite as Mike and I gave him a talking to.

'You've got off to a bad start, there, son,' Mike told him. 'And you need to think hard about behaving, or else this holiday won't be a bundle of fun for any of us, will it? You understand?'

Justin nodded glumly, looking green.

He wasn't on points while we were away, so there were none of those sorts of sanctions, but there was a system in place whereby all three of the children would get ten euros a day to spend on whatever they fancied. But it was absolutely conditional on good behaviour. 'So any more kicking off,' Mike said sternly, 'and you can wave goodbye to your pocket money. You got that?'

'I've got that,' said Justin.

Truth was that he was looking so ill by now – and feeling pretty sick with it – that we felt he was already learning his lesson anyway. First night hiccup, we both agreed. Perhaps a symptom of over-excitement. Things would be just fine in the morning, as long as we kept things low key and didn't try to introduce too much in the way of new experiences. A quiet day around the pool would do the trick.

* * *

Sadly, however, our confident prediction didn't happen, as the next day began as the night before had ended, with Justin in a stupendously unpleasant mood. He just seemed incapable of behaving himself from the outset and continued to be aggressive and unpleasant all day. He seemed to find it highly amusing to hold Chloe's head under the water until she was spluttering for breath and despite our remonstrations kept returning to the same dangerous game, to the point where Chloe had had enough and was really upset.

I was just trying to comfort her when a commotion nearby made us turn to see that Justin had pushed two young children into the water, and was simply standing there watching, completely relaxed, as they both thrashed around desperately in the water.

The children's father, once he got them out, was completely furious, as he would be, and it took Mike quite a while to calm him down. Then, needing to be seen to be properly disciplining his wayward offspring, he rounded on Justin. 'Right!' he said, 'that's *enough*!'

Justin just stood there and blinked at him for a second, then, right on cue, spat out a heartfelt and very voluble 'Fucking leave me alone!' before swinging around and cantering off out of the pool complex.

'Great,' said Mike, reaching for his flip-flops. 'Just great.'

I got up off my sun-bed and wriggled my feet into my own, grabbing my sarong and my bag as I did so. Once again we were at the centre of some impromptu light entertainment – I could feel every eye in the place, screened behind the safety of sunglasses, swivelled and fixed in our direction. And the spectators included my niece and nephew, who were still in the pool themselves, and who now transferred their gazes to the general direction of Justin's exit, their 'What *now*?' expressions a picture.

I turned to Riley. 'Keep an eye on Chloe and Daniel, will you, love?'

She rolled her eyes and nodded. 'Best of luck …' Mike and I trotted off in pursuit.

It took us a good hour to find Justin. An hour in which I went through every possible emotion, from wanting to throttle him, to feeling guilty that we'd misjudged his state of progress so badly, cursing him over the blister I could feel forming between my toes, to feeling that gut-churning fear that you get if you mislay a toddler, to wanting to throttle him again. It was a hot afternoon and we were very quickly footsore, as we trudged up and down the prome-nade, in and out of side-streets, and over broad sweeps of beach, our eyes constantly scanning the face of every curly blond head we could see.

I knew that both the pavements and the sand would be hot, and he was barefoot, so maybe, I suggested, he would have worked his way back now. Perhaps I should call Riley and have her go check our apartments We had two; she was sharing with Chloe and Daniel, and Mike, Justin and I had the other one. Maybe by now, having grown weary of the heat, he'd headed to the latter to cool off. I was just pulling my bag from my shoulder to get my phone out when Mike's arm suddenly flew out. 'There he is!'

Justin was nearby on the prom – no more than 200 yards from the hotel – standing at the entrance to an amusement arcade. I was naturally not in the best of moods by now, and rounded on him angrily as soon as we got to him.

'I'm *so* cross with you, Justin!' I snapped at him angrily. 'How *dare* you do that! How dare you –'

But I didn't get to finish. He span straight around and ran away again.

'Justin!' yelled Mike, who was every bit as annoyed as I was. 'Justin, just you come back this *minute!*'

But it seemed that destiny was listening, even if Justin wasn't, because just at the point when we'd both broken into a jog – with Justin some forty yards distant from us already, and the gap opening – he decided to turn around and check if we were still in pursuit. And not having eyes in the back of his head, he ran, full pelt, smack into a palm tree.

I gasped in horror because he bounced – he really bounced. Flew backwards and then went down like a skittle. He could have broken his nose easily, cracked his skull open – anything. At the very least, I half-expected to get to him and find he was minus his front teeth.

But by the time we both got to him, he was already scrambling to his feet, and seeing us, he suddenly burst out laughing. As did Mike and I, too – all in a mad rush. We couldn't help it. And though our own laughter was probably slightly hysterical as much as anything, it was as if, in that instant, the whole tone had been reset, and this slapstick event had really changed Justin's mood.

We didn't expect it, didn't even dare hope for it, as we trudged back, but from that afternoon on there wasn't another cross word required. The rest of the holiday went brilliantly.

Chapter 18

'Spaghetti bolognaise!' Justin announced with an excited flourish. 'I'm gonna make-a the best-a bolognaise-a you ever tasted!'

I grinned at him as he reached for the pen and paper I'd given him. It was a Wednesday afternoon, and we were sitting in the conservatory with a pile of recipe books spread out on the floor in front of us, from which Justin was going to choose a recipe so he could make us a special meal.

Almost as soon as we'd returned from holiday, it had been time for Justin to be moved up to the final level of his points programme. He'd now completed all the components that were part of level two, and had amassed sufficient points to move up. Level three came with a new set of more subtle and challenging targets, as well as a new set of rewards.

He was now expected to demonstrate such complex social skills as showing respect for other people's feelings, and doing something nice for someone, daily, and without prompting, as well as having more rigorous standards applied to his education; to earn his points, he had to read for an hour daily, for example – something that might challenge even the most biddable of twelve-year-old boys.

His rewards, too, were more complex, and I was thrilled to see how much he was motivated by them. There was still the issue of friendship-based rewards, of course, because since the incident with Gregory he seemed to have made little in the way of further friendships and still struggled to interact positively with his peers. But the rest of the rewards were essentially family-orientated, and he really worked hard to attain them – things like organising a big family DVD night for all the family, with popcorn and fizzy drinks and pizza and so on, and his favourite – pretty obvious, given his main preoccupation – which involved choosing and preparing a special meal for us all.

'That sounds *bellissimo*,' I told him now. 'And we'd better get cracking. It's almost four already and we still need to get to the shops.'

It had been a tense couple of days, so I was glad we had something so positive to do together. Though he'd been welcomed back into school, it was hardly with open arms. Indeed, on the first day, it had been made clear – by a committee comprising a representative of the board of governors, the head and the special educational needs co-ordinator – that this was definitely going to be the last chance for Justin, before emergency measures were put in place.

He basically had to sign a behavioural contract. For the school's part, he would be given extra support in lessons and would always be accompanied during transitions from class to class. He would also have the option of spending break times inside the learning-support classroom, and would be allowed to go on the computers in there. For his part, he had to commit to maintaining good behaviour, which he was actually quite happy about, since he loved computers. A carrot rather than stick approach, and the right one.

The two of us made the trip to the supermarket right away, him armed with the shopping list he had now carefully written out himself, having consulted the recipe book he'd chosen it from. He loved Jamie Oliver. In fact the celebrity chef was something of a hero to Justin; he reckoned being a chef was the best job in the world, and often told us that one day he too would be on TV too, whipping up amazing meals while playing the clown, just like Jamie. We'd bought him the book from Tesco as soon as he'd mentioned it to us, and he'd often sit looking at it while I prepared dinner, telling me about all the fabulous meals he was also one day going to invent.

The tension of the upcoming return to school notwithstanding, I'd been in a pretty buoyant mood since we'd returned from the holiday as it seemed to mark a real turning point in so many aspects of Justin's behaviour. They say a change is as good as rest – even if that wasn't true for our Kieron – and though no-one would suggest that a week in the sunshine was any sort of panacea for a boy with such troubles, there did seem something so much less uptight about him lately, which made everything at home so much calmer. Of course, it might have been nothing more than a coincidence of timing, but I didn't much care. I was just so glad we'd turned a corner.

By the time we arrived back at the house, Kieron was already home from college and I knew Mike – always starving after his usual physically punishing days – would not be too far behind him, as well as Riley and David, who were coming to dinner also, to sample Justin's first made-it-all by-myself meal.

Jamie Oliver might have not yet written his *30 Minute Meals* at this time, but if he had, I'm sure Justin would have managed just fine. He was hilarious, and Kieron and I were almost crying with laughter as he adopted a Cockney accent and proceeded to do the whole thing in role. 'Lavverly, this'll be, may-tey!' he said as he chopped mushrooms. Chopped them with skill and aplomb, too, I noted. His culinary ambitions weren't a pipe dream, I realised. He had definite passion and a great deal of flair.

'And now,' he went on, 'jast a *leetle* pinch of pepper. An' look at that! Bluddy marvellous that is! Pukka!'

At that point, I heard the door and Riley and David both appeared. 'Ah!' cried Justin, when he saw them, with a theatrical flourish. 'Two more audience members in! Laaaavverly! At the front please, madam!' he said, waving an expansive arm towards Riley. 'Get the lady a seat, sir!' he then ordered David. By the time Mike walked through the door we really were all in stitches, so much so that he wondered what on earth had been going on.

For most people, I remember thinking, this would be quite unremarkable. Just a family, messing about, having fun, having a laugh. But for Justin, this was *huge*. This was the sort of stuff he'd never had. And at the same time a pertinent reminder to me and Mike that it was this – this constant and reassuring normality – that underpinned everything we did as foster parents.

And it was so wonderful to see Justin coming out of his shell. So good to see him feeling relaxed and secure enough to be the centre of attention, and for the best of reasons rather than the worst. Clearly, underneath the skin of this sad and troubled boy lurked the soul of a true and gifted comic. So as I stood there and laughed I was also crying a bit inside – it just seemed so random and damning a thing that a child could be born into the sort of conditions that so effectively snuffed out every tiny flicker of potential they had. Random and tragic but I hoped still repairable, even if teasing out the true child inside was going to be such a long and daunting task.

And within a couple of weeks, the task would get harder.

One of the new things Justin was currently engaged in was a search to see if he could try and trace his father. This had come about, by chance, as a result of the holiday. Once I'd finally got around to getting the photos printed, I'd had the idea of making a few copies for Justin, so he could put them in his memory box.

We were sitting in his bedroom, going through them – I'd just brought them up to him – and he was laughing at them, one by one, reliving all the happy memories, when he came upon a particularly nice one of him and Mike – the two of them, posing in front of a pool, ready to go scuba diving. Mike had his arm draped around Justin's shoulders and they were both smiling broadly. He transferred it to the box and then said, without any sort of prompting, 'If anyone asks me, you know, like, if I leave here, I'll just tell them that's me and me dad.'

I felt a lump form in my throat – a real physical pang. Swallowing it (get a grip, woman, I told myself sternly), I then thought about how stable things had been at home just lately, and how this might be a good point to broach the subject of his real dad. It had been something that had only really come up in passing since he'd been with us, and had previously seemed to be something well left. He'd only ever really mentioned a couple of names his mum and nan had told him of, and it had seemed to me that he had quite enough on his plate dealing with the relatives he *did* know about, let alone trying to find another to let him down.

But something told me that now might be the moment to bring it up again. After all, if we were going to piece together his background in any useful way, we needed all the pieces of the jigsaw in place. After all, even if this one was going to prove a dead end, it would be better than remaining a question.

'Why not?' I answered brightly, reassuring him that it would be just fine by us. 'He's a kind of dad, after all. He's your foster dad, isn't he? And I think he'd like that.' Justin grinned, seemingly pleased with my answer. 'But you know what?' I continued. 'Have you thought about your real dad? You know, there's nothing to stop us doing some detective work, if you want to. You know, ask Harrison Green to look into things for you.'

This seemed to animate him, and it was clear that this was something he did think about, even if it wasn't something we'd discussed before.

'I'd like to know,' he said, nodding. 'Because there's two names that's come up. I been told loads of lies about it by me mum, and me nan, too, but there's two names that have kept coming up all the time. One man, me nan says, wouldn't even know I exist because if it was him, me mum never even told him she was pregnant. It could be one of them, couldn't it?'

I nodded. 'I guess it could.' I turned a little on the bed so that I could look at him directly. 'Though you have to understand, love, that it might not lead to anything. You know – not get your hopes up too much about it, because even if we find him, it doesn't necessarily mean he wants to "be" a dad to you.'

'I know that,' he said solemnly. 'An' that's fine. Just be nice to know, wouldn't it?'

'Yes,' I said, 'Yes, it would.'

I telephoned both Harrison Green and John Fulshaw the next morning, the former to see if he could start to do some digging, and the latter just because I wanted to keep him in the loop. Later on that day, Harrison called back and confirmed that social services did indeed have a couple of names on file. He seemed surprised, saying that Justin had never brought this up with him, so I filled him in on the photos and my prompting, and shared my thoughts on why it seemed important to try and establish as many facts as we could, because I thought it was important for Justin's emotional wellbeing. I thought of adding – but didn't say, as I was getting to grips with my role now – that perhaps at some point he could have asked.

But he did make the effort, because he called again two days later, this time to tell me he had news to impart, and suggesting we all go for a burger. There was never a time when Justin would willingly turn down a burger, so we arranged to head to town the following afternoon, straight after school, so that Harrison could fill us in with what he'd learned.

'You're certainly right that there's two possibles,' he confirmed, matter of factly, once we'd got the essential business of the food out of the way.

I was struck, as I always was, by his slightly detached tone; this feeling of him not giving either Justin or me his full attention. I might have misinterpreted it, but I always had this sense about Harrison that we were very much one of a big pile of files on his desk, and that he always had half his mind on one of the others at the same time. And it looked like he wasn't about to let me down in that regard.

'Only got an address for one of them, though,' he added, 'which is probably a good thing.' His brow furrowed slightly. 'Probably better if it's not the other one, to be honest – because from what I've heard, asking around, he's a bit of a wrong 'un, Justin. Could possibly be in jail, even, as it happens.'

I was, to put it mildly, astounded by his lack of tact – did he really think it the right thing to say straight out, in front of Justin? Where did that leave him if it turned out the possible jailbird *did* turn out to be his dad? Really helpful, that, I thought. But I bit my tongue and said nothing, because there was no point – the deed was already done.

And Justin himself, it had to be said, was altogether more interested in the other one anyway – the one Harrison had tracked down to an address about twenty miles away, and who he was already getting excited about meeting. I could see his mind whirring, even as he munched on his burger, creating whole father-and-son scenarios out of this small nugget of news. I so hoped he wasn't going to have his hopes crushed by all this, yet what were the chances of that not being so? This potential dad, I imagined, either had not the least inkling of his existence, as he predicted, or knew full well who he was and had no interest in him at all. And even if it were the former and the man accepted his paternity, what were the chances, given the world Justin's mother lived in, that he'd say 'Hurrah! I have a son!' and welcome him into his life with open arms? About a zillion to one would be my best estimate. If that was going to happen, surely it would have happened several years back? So I, for one, wasn't holding my breath.

But this wasn't just about that – wonderful though it might be. It was mostly about putting together all the pieces of his past. Justin's being able to piece together the details of where he came from was never going to be a bad thing; who doesn't want to know how they got here, however difficult the circumstances? So I kept positive for his sake and my fingers firmly crossed.

And there was no let-up in Justin's excitement. He was watching *EastEnders* that evening with Mike and me, and the Mitchell brothers were up to their usual antics.

'I wonder if he's going to be big and hard like Phil Mitchell,' he wondered. 'I bet he is, Mike, don't you?'

Mike nodded. 'He could well be. After all, you're a big lad, aren't you?'

'Yes, he is, love,' I said to Mike. 'He definitely is. But don't forget, Justin, there's always a chance that this man *isn't* your dad.'

I hated having to see the look of frustration cross Justin's face, and also that I had to play devil's advocate. It was me, after all, that had got this ball rolling. But, at the same time, I didn't want it rolling out of control. I shot Mike a warning glance, and he seemed to understand. As, I think, did Justin, once he gave it a second's thought. 'I know that, Casey, I really do, honest. I'm just saying that if it *is* my dad, he *will* probably be big.'

'Possibly love, yes. But it doesn't matter anyway, does it, because the one thing we do know is that, whoever he is, he's going to be good looking. How could he not be? What with having such a looker for a son.' I reached across the sofa then, to tickle him. 'What with all those blond curly ringlets.'

* * *

The next call came from Harrison only twenty-four hours later. He'd apparently spoken to the man in question that morning, and he'd agreed to meet Justin 'for a chat'.

But this conversation was with me, and not Justin, for which I was grateful, because it seemed Harrison wasn't holding his breath either.

'I don't actually know what'll come of it,' he told me. 'Because the man sounds more interested in *not* being Justin's dad. Told me he'd know straight away if Justin was one of his. Said all his other children look alike.'

Like he was siring dogs for Crufts, I thought, but didn't say. How very nice.

But, if anything, it was Justin who reassured me.

'Don't worry, Casey,' he told me, as I gave him his fifth 'Don't get your hopes up' lecture. 'It's not like I have any feelings for him or anything. I don't *know* him, do I? So if he's not my dad, then it don't matter, do it? It's *fine*.'

We couldn't go with Justin, obviously, because that was outside our remit. It was arranged that Harrison Green would come round and pick up, and then take him down to the snooker hall in the town centre, which was the agreed location of the meeting. It was hard to articulate my feelings as I waved them both off. I was just aware of this knot of anxiety inside me, which I couldn't shake for the hour or so the two of them were gone.

Mike returned home in the interim, and I recalled that I'd felt something similar when Kieron had started secondary school. He'd been so proud that he was going, but I knew that at the same time he was terrified. Terrified of the sheer size of the place, the vast numbers of other children, the overwhelming nature of everything; so many people and so much noise. I'd felt physically ill all day for him, and by the time he came home, I had bitten all my nails to the quick.

I told Mike – I'd already told him what Justin had said to me about the photo – and I realised it wasn't just me that felt this fierce need to protect him.

'But, love,' he said, '*we're* here for him. And what he said to you is right. There's never been a father in his life, don't forget. So it's not like this man can hurt him any more than he's already *been* hurt. Sure, if it doesn't work out, he's going to be disappointed, but disappointed is not the same as heartbroken, is it? He's enough on his plate in that department, dealing with his bloody mum.'

So I tried to be mollified and tried not to worry, but I still couldn't help but feel my heart going out to him, having to go to a strange place, meet a strange man and to have to ask him, 'Are you my dad?' Should any child have to do that? No, they shouldn't.

And I knew, just as soon as I saw Justin and Harrison walking back up the front path, that the whole thing had actually been fruitless.

'So, love,' I asked him, as I quickly toasted crumpets. Harrison had declined my offer of a cup of tea, thankfully, so it was just the three of us now in the kitchen. 'How did it go, then? What was he like?'

Justin cupped his hands around a steaming mug of hot chocolate. 'He was alright,' he said, frowning. 'But I was, like, dead nervous, Casey. I walked in, like, and I didn't have a clue what to say. He was massive, too, and a bit fat, and I bet I'm gonna take after him.' He didn't qualify as to whether this would be a good thing or a bad thing. I could only go by his expression, which told me nothing.

'Anyway,' Justin went on. 'He just goes, "Alright, lad? You want to play a game of snooker or something?" So we had a game, and, like, I let him win, because he's my dad and that …' Mike and I now exchanged glances. 'An' he bought me a Coke – sorry, Casey, he didn't know I'm not allowed it.'

'But you do, you cheeky monkey! But no matter now, I suppose. Go on. What happened then?'

'Well we just sat for a bit …' He grinned now, obviously remembering. 'Like two old men sat in a pub we were, the pair of us. Then he goes to me, like, "It's been good today, lad, and all that." And then, "And to be honest, lad, I still don't even know if I *am* your dad."'

'And then?' asked Mike gently.

'An' that was it, really. He said I needed to know that he'd got his own family now and that him and my mum were, like, *years* ago. He said he didn't even really remember her. An' then he said that that was, like, as far as it goes. And then he said sorry …' Justin now picked up his crumpet and looked at it. I could see that, little by little, this was becoming more and more painful. Just the action of recounting it was hammering it home. 'He said he was sorry,' he finished, before taking his first bite, 'but he already had enough on his plate.'

Mike and I were silent for only a short second, but it was a deep heavy silence even so.

'It's okay, sweetheart,' I said, pulling out a chair between them at the table, and sitting down. 'But at least you finally got to meet him – at least you can put a face to him now. Far better, that, than not knowing, eh?'

'And he did the right thing,' added Mike, reaching out to pat Justin's arm. 'He took the time and trouble to come and see you at least.'

'Exactly,' I agreed, though inside I was so sad for him, having it pointed out so baldly that he was a child who had simply been replaced.

'I suppose so,' Justin said, and, again, I couldn't read him. 'Though he did say, if ever I needed a kidney or owt … But I think he was joking, don't you?'

Chapter 19

Though we didn't know for sure (and, as it turned out, we never did find out) who Justin's father was, the business of looking for him had sparked a new enthusiasm in Justin to sit down and really get to grips with where he came from and who he was now.

This was a major step on the road to unravelling the tangle of dark thoughts and memories in his young head and would, I knew, be an important part of the process we started when he came to us. It also seemed a sensible idea to unravel things, literally. To sit down and make a chart of his life, in date order, so he could look back with clarity at what had gone before. He's always been quite vague about where he'd been and when, which wasn't surprising, given the number of placements he'd been through, which also meant he would often get confused about dates and names.

It was a Saturday afternoon, and we had the house to ourselves, while Kieron and Mike were at football, so I suggested Justin bring down his memory box and that we start creating a personal timeline for him.

'Like you might have done at primary school,' I said, thinking back to find a good analogy. 'Do you remember those ones they do in class on a long, long strip of paper, to explain how the earth was made? Where you start at the beginning of time and work forwards, putting in the creation of the mountains, and then the first life beginning in the sea, and then the dinosaurs –'

'And with humans right at the very end, like, for only *this* much?' Justin pinched finger and thumb together to indicate a tiny distance. 'Because we've only been here for such a tiny amount of time?'

'That's the one!' I said. 'So you were obviously listening, then!'

I'd been feeling quite emotional since the business with Justin's dad, as it had really hit home to me just how grim his life had been. I'd been lying in bed on the night of the meeting, unable to sleep (as Mike remarked, nothing new there, then), and had been saying how awful it was that, apart from his little brothers, who would probably end up losing contact with him anyway, there wasn't a single person out there who loved him. It upset me so much, that; to think of it in those terms. To embrace the enormity of having to live in a world where there's no-one who cares if you're happy or sad, whether you're well or feeling down or making your way or need a hug. It was so far from my own experience, with our huge loving family, that it was difficult to take in as a concept. I tried to explain it all to Mike, who lay and listened to me whispering, then turned and said, 'But, Case, he has *us* now, at least'.

'I know, but –' I started to say in reply.

'And *we* love him, don't we? You and me,' he whispered back.

And he was right. Yes we did. He had us now.

Once I'd explained the concept to Justin, and how we'd go about making a timeline just for him, we both went into the garage and, after a short rummage, found what I knew was in there somewhere. A big roll of leftover wallpaper from way back – from when we last decorated Kieron's bedroom.

We took it into the dining room, and set to work to make sufficient space to do it, moving the dining table and chairs and stacking the latter against the opposite wall, so we had plenty of big empty floor and wall space. 'This is a hell of a lot of paper,' Justin observed, holding one end up as I balled bits of Blu-Tack and stuck them to the back of it.

'That's because,' I said, grinning, as I fixed my end to the wall, 'you've had one hell of a lot of life, love.'

It turned out to be a long old process. We started with his birth, which he carefully wrote at one end of the timeline – he'd bought his pencil case of coloured felt pens down from his bedroom for the purpose, as well as his memory box of mementoes – and then moved forwards, year by year.

Right from the off, I realised this would be no simple task. Justin had an awful lot of gaps in his memory, and really struggled, initially, with the order in which we were doing things. It really hit home when I glanced at the time, hearing the front door open. We'd been at it for three hours already by that time, and on our timeline he was still only six years old.

With Mike and Kieron home, I took the opportunity to suggest a break for tea. This was turning out to be a bigger job than I realised.

While I went into the kitchen to knock up some drinks and a round of sandwiches, I could hear Justin explaining to Kieron and Mike exactly what it was we were trying to achieve.

'Only it's hard,' he was saying, because I keep getting confused. It's such a long time back, being six.

'Even longer for me, mate,' I heard Mike observe. 'Perhaps,' he lowered his voice here, in a theatrical manner, 'Casey's had you go about it the wrong way. Tell you what I'd do if it was me trying to remember. I'd forget putting up dates; I'd just work with ages. Start with the things you definitely remember when you were whatever years old. Then you can go though that lot [he obviously meant Justin's memory box] and start by sticking up all the things you can be sure of the date of – that photo for instance, and that ticket stub – see? That's dated – and once you've got all that up and in definite order then it's just a case of filling in the gaps.'

By the time I came in, with my tray full of cheese and ham sandwiches, they'd made more progress in fifteen minutes than we had all afternoon.

I smiled gratefully at Mike. What would I ever do without him? We were away again and storming along straight after tea.

And it was such a positive thing to do because, rather than keep focussing on the negative, using Justin's happy memories and mementoes made us focus on the good times, reminding him that there were chinks of light amid the darkness and that, actually, there were a lot of good people in the world.

'Oh, yes!' he'd enthuse. 'That was when I was living with the Phillips family, and I went to St Cuthbert's and had this friend, Tom.' Then his face would light up and he'd be off on another memory, excitedly telling me about something good that had happened instead of painfully recounting something bad.

Listening to him, I suddenly realised how absolutely crucial these memory boxes were, and how right social services were to insist that each foster carer had to record all memorable events in a child's life. Without the photos and mementoes, we could have never done this, and it was so enlightening and therapeutic to see. I remembered how, in my training, I'd been told that children often resented their memory boxes – saw them as a sad reminder of unhappy times. That may have been so, but at times like this, when a child was obviously ready to address such things, it really was a vital piece of kit.

As we continued with the marathon bout of sticking and note-writing, we were able to talk about relatives that Justin had never even mentioned: aunties and uncles and even several cousins. So without him even realising what he was doing, he was actually extending his family and placing himself in a far wider support circle. Someone, somewhere within social services, obviously knew what they were doing when they came up with the idea of memory boxes.

But the bad memories were, of course, every bit as important as the good, because the process of taking ownership of these previous suppressed memories was vital to his emotional wellbeing and, at one point, when talking about his nanna, his mum's mum, he suddenly came out with a comment about his mum that really proved just how far he'd come.

'I know drugs are wrong,' he said. 'But I can also kind of see why she did it. Because no-one stopped her. Because my nanna never really cared what she did.'

'Did your mum tell you that?' I asked him. He nodded. 'Yeah, she did. She said she was left by herself all the time, pretty much. So her mates would come round and they'd smoke weed.'

So simple, I thought. And so depressingly telling. From such small beginnings do whole lives get destroyed.

* * *

Completing the timeline ended up taking up most of that weekend, and it was immediately obvious that it had proved cathartic for Justin. It was as if it had opened up a new seam of memories; memories, moreover, that Justin wanted to share.

We were having our usual Sunday roast the following weekend, around the middle of September, with the whole family there, including David and a now very heavily pregnant Riley, and we'd just finished eating our dessert. Conversation had turned at that point to something topical that had been on *EastEnders* that week, as it often did, as we were all fans. I don't recall the exact storyline, but I think it was something about drug abuse, prompting Justin to comment about his mum 'doing drugs' and how he remembered how scary it had been.

'I was about seven,' he said, brow furrowing. 'Something like that.'

I recalled the timeline. So this would have been one of the intermittent short periods when he was back with his mum and his brothers. 'I was upstairs,' he went on. 'It was evening, I think. Night time. And I didn't know where she was, so I went downstairs to find her. An' she was lying on the floor in the living room, on the rug, and it was like she was dead. I couldn't wake her up.' We were all riveted now, of course, listening intently. 'I kept shouting at her and shaking her and she just didn't move. And then I saw this needle, and it was just sticking out of her arm, and I was really frightened, so I went to get Paul.'

'Your next door neighbour?' I asked him. He nodded.

'Yes, Paul. And he came back with me and put her in the bath. Just pulled the needle out and picked her up and carried her upstairs, and put her in the bath, with her still with all her clothes on.

'An' then he just kept slapping her in the face until she woke up. An' then, when he was trying to get her back out of the bath again, she threw up all over herself. There was sick everywhere – *everywhere*. All over her clothes, all over the lino. An' then, when she moved, I saw there was poo running down the insides of her legs, too.'

We were all, I think, too stunned to speak as he said this, the horrible images all clamouring to fill our heads. It was a pretty grisly scene to see from anyone's perspective, let alone that of an impressionable seven-year-old child. And this wasn't just anyone, either, of course. It was his *mother* that Justin had seen in this state.

'Oh, love, 'I said, finally. 'What a thing to have to witness. No wonder you were so frightened. I'm sure anyone would have been.'

Justin shrugged. 'But you know, it was strange,' he said thoughtfully. 'It was like it was all happening. But kind of *not*, at the same time. It was almost like I was watching it on TV.'

It was always like that for him, he went on to tell us. Like he was watching his own life, like he was a character in a movie. And that the things that were happening weren't happening to him.

'It's like I've only just worked it out – that they *did* happen to me. It's weird,' he finished. 'I can't really explain it.'

Riley, in particular, had grown really upset now, and twin tracks of tears were running unchecked down her cheeks. It had happened so stealthily that I had almost not seen it happen, but I realised just how fond she had grown of Justin, and he of her. She was also pregnant, and, in common with almost every other pregnant woman ever, she was thinking about the child she had growing inside her, and was very sensitive to the idea of *any* child being hurt. She stood up, came round the table and threw her arms around Justin, saying nothing. And, more to the point, he let her embrace him without flinching. Even inched his arms around her, too.

It was very moving to watch, and also a huge break-through. And later, when I tucked Justin in, I spent some time in his bedroom, explaining to him that this was how the mind sometimes worked. It protected you from things that would cause you great distress, by shutting you off a little, detaching you enough so you could cope. I also told him that his being able to understand that that had happened was a clear indicator that he was beginning to make a recovery and, because of that, he could begin the process of accepting these things were real.

And the change in Justin wasn't just emotional. There was a physical change too, a very visible one. It was if a mask had been removed now, a whole layer of worry. It was like he was finally learning to cope with being Justin, and to take ownership, finally, of his harrowing past.

He was also beginning to apply himself at school, which was a wonderful indicator of how far he'd come.

But there was still a way to go; still so much help that was needed if he was going to be equipped to face the future and, in that, we felt sure we *could* make a difference – just as long as we continued as we were.

We crossed our fingers, too. After all, it couldn't hurt.

Chapter 20

It was now late September and I was beginning to get excited. Riley was almost 37 weeks pregnant, and blooming, and the birth – for so long an event on the far horizon – was rushing headlong to meet us. I couldn't wait. It seemed incredible, looking back, just how eventful a year we'd been having; starting a whole new career, and taking in Justin, and in the midst of it all my darling daughter and her lovely partner had been quietly having a small revolution of their own, bringing Mike and my first grandchild into the world.

And like any prospective new grandparents, we couldn't have been more excited. I'd gone with Riley to almost all of her antenatal appointments, her midwife very sweetly arranging all of them to suit me, bless her, knowing I could only attend when Justin was in school. We had the first scan photo proudly affixed to the kitchen fridge and, upstairs, in our bedroom, Mike and I had quite a baby collection going, from a new pram and a state of the art sterilising unit to an ever growing collection of baby clothes.

Mike had also planned to surprise Riley when she came out of hospital by whizzing in while she was in there and decorating the room she was going to use for the baby's nursery. He'd hatched his plan because David had commented that they couldn't really afford to sort the nursery out straight away, and had said that they intended to keep the baby in with them until they'd got enough time and money to get around to it. So the new granddad-to-be had taken himself shopping, and bought Winnie the Pooh wallpaper, borders and soft toys, all of which he had now hidden until the big day. It would be a big job to do in what was likely to be a small space of time, but if anyone could do it, I knew Mike could.

But there was something else looming – also on the near horizon – and, in contrast to the impending birth of Riley's baby, this was one thing I wasn't looking forward to at all. At some point, quite soon now, the time would come for Justin to leave us, and move to the new foster placement that my fostering agency had been planning for and quietly putting in place since day one.

I should have been prepared, of course, because I'd always known this. Our kind of fostering – indeed, in truth, *any* kind of fostering – was never designed to be permanent. But like anyone whose preference was to live in the moment, as mine was, I'd tried not to think about the longer-term plans with anything other than an optimistic bent. This worked well when things were bad, and would work well when we let him go, but right now, the only thing I really didn't want to think about was the fact that he would soon have to join a new family.

It was brought home to me forcibly one quiet weekday evening when he and I, as had become our habit, almost without my really noticing, were sitting together on the sofa, watching telly.

Mike had gone up to have a bath and Justin, who'd been sitting at the other end of the sofa, now snuggled up and put his head in my lap.

I smiled as I began stroking the soft curls away from his forehead. Like so much else, this physical closeness, as natural as breathing to most children and their parents, and so alien to Justin when he'd come to us, had kind of crept up without us really noticing.

'You'll soon be too big,' I said, 'to want to do this with me any more, sunshine.'

He grinned up at me. 'So you'd better make the most of it, then!'

I laughed as he turned back to the TV and made himself comfortable. 'Ten minutes then,' I said. 'Then I have to get up and make Mike's supper.'

'Okay,' he said, 'but Casey?'

'Mmm?'

'I'll never really be too big for this, will I? Not *really*. Because it's like I'm your *real* son now, isn't it? And *real* sons never get too big for snuggling up to their mum, do they?'

'No babes,' I agreed. 'No, they don't.'

I was so, so moved, and also, despite its bittersweet nature, also quietly thrilled by what Justin had said – could there honestly be a greater affirmation that we'd made progress? But at the same time I felt the waves of sadness wash over me. This was also proof that our job was almost done.

We'd covered this at some length in training. The programme was designed so that over a year, give or take, the child would go through, and pass, all the stages of the treatment, and hopefully arrive at the end of the process both practically and emotionally ready to move on – and back, hopefully, into mainstream foster care. This wasn't always going to happen of course (as Mike and I would find out with other children, when we were further down the line) but, if it worked, that was always the ultimate goal. No-one ever wanted to see a child in care essentially given up on, so it mattered to everyone involved in both its intro-duction and its provision that the programme was so far registering lots of successes.

I stood in the kitchen, that evening, watching Justin sitting beside me at the table, quietly finishing off a of piece of homework, and tried to imagine our lives once again without him.

I had spent a long time during training trying to imagine making the difficult transition from free and easy parents of independent grown children to responsible carers for pubescents and young teens again – how would we adapt to once again losing our freedom? How well would we cope again with tears and tantrums? How would we get on, constantly doling out discipline? But now we'd done that it struck me that I'd never once considered how difficult it would be to let go of the child. You saw your own children through life – right from the cradle to adulthood and beyond. This was so different, like handing over a job not yet done.

But our part *was* done, and we had to accept it. More worrying, though, was would *he*? He was a damaged child, badly hurt, and as we'd been told, over and over, damaged children tend to block out things that cause them any pain. So it was difficult to know how he would take this new change: would he regress to old ways of behaving in order to deal with it?

One thing that had been emphasised during our training was that we should expect, once the process of moving on had been started, a regression in Justin's behaviour. It didn't matter how clear it had been made to him at the beginning of the process that this was a temporary placement, with a specific goal in mind – *another* placement – he would, we were promised, have blocked that out. And what might happen, John had told us, now the reality of that was about to stare him in the face, was an almost inevitable negative response.

In short, he would not want to leave us. And why would he? He'd just told me he felt happy and like one of the family – *our* family. How cruel life could be. I felt awful.

And it must have been affecting me more than I realised, because while on autopilot, preparing veg for dinner while he worked, I found myself reaching into the cupboard for a pack of crumpets and the hot chocolate. Our Friday treat, and it wasn't even Friday.

Once I'd had a chat with John about Justin having reached the end of the points programme, things began to move quickly.

'We need to set up a meeting,' he told me. 'All of us. You and Mike, obviously, plus Harrison and I, so we can sit down and explain everything in detail to Justin. We've found a family – we've both met them – who we feel are pretty perfect, and once we've told Justin about them, we want to go ahead and arrange for them all to meet. But brace yourself, Casey,' he warned. 'This is the tough bit.'

'It feels like it,' I said. 'And the "bit" hasn't even happened yet!' I laughed, but it was only on the outside. 'I'm dreading telling him,' I confessed. 'I'm dreading seeing his expression.'

'I'm sure it won't be as bad as you imagine,' John counselled.

I was equally sure it probably would be. I looked back – the 'Little Mermaid' pool party, the holiday in Spain, the small triumphs, the big disasters, the trust he'd finally placed in us. The love.

How did you tell a child that he was going to have to vacate the very bedroom that he had at last come to see as his principal place of safety? How did you tell a child he had to leave you, full stop?

I'd had many wobbles on the journey Mike and I had embarked on in all this. Both before it, and during training, and many, many times since. But they were as nothing to the wobble I was having now.

Chapter 21

'Aw, it's not fair. I soooo want to come!' Riley pulled a face as she plonked herself down at the kitchen table. Bob immediately came up and licked her hand, as if sympathising with her evident dismay.

Bob had been back with us for a while now, both Kieron and Lauren having made the decision that Justin was mature enough to behave himself around him. And it had been a good decision. The two of them were now pretty much inseparable, but along with that it was clear the Justin also understood that Bob was a family pet, to be loved by all the family.

'I know, love,' I said. 'And we're all going to miss you. But look at you – you could go into labour at any moment.'

'Exactly,' agreed Justin, pulling his new hoodie over his head. We'd been out and chosen a brand new set of clothes for him. New trainers, some natty joggers and a pillar-box-red zip-up hoodie. 'Supposing your waters break all over the car seat? YEUUCH!!'

'Well, that's charming,' huffed Riley.

'Yes, gross, mate!' agreed Kieron.

'Yes, delightful,' agreed Mike, his grin almost as wide as mine was. 'But come on, you lovely lot. It's getting late. Time to go.'

It was two weeks into October now and we were all off on an adventure. Well, bar Riley, of course, now 39 weeks pregnant and currently so huge that both her doctor and midwife had advised her against going pretty much *anywhere*, as they felt she could go into labour at any moment. But the rest of us were off to the ceremony that would mark Justin's graduation from the specialist foster programme. It was a very big day for him, and pretty special for us, too – we were all of us first timers at this.

The ceremony was to take place in the function suite of the team offices for our fostering agency, and everyone involved in Justin's care would be there. We were all gutted Riley couldn't be with us to share the moment, but, actually, the potential situation Justin so delicately outlined would, if it happened, cause big problems. It was a good hour's drive away and, if she did go into labour, she'd have one hell of a long journey back to hospital.

We arrived at around eleven, after a trouble-free journey, and right away I could see how seriously they took the whole business – and rightly so, to my mind; the children the course was intended for were the sort of kids for whom success at *anything* was a very big deal indeed. It was right and proper that they learned that what you put in you could definitely get out in this life, and I smiled at the red carpet that had been laid at the entrance to the function suite, albeit optimistically, given the leaden October sky – why shouldn't our lad be a star for the day?

Even so, I was still really moved to see just how *much* of an effort the staff at the agency had made. As well as the red carpet there was a huge golden banner hanging above the doorway, too, which said 'Well Done Justin – You Did It!' in huge lettering. I made a mental note to be sure to take a photo of it before we left.

'Oh, my God, Casey! Look at that!' Justin said, gasping as he saw it. 'Aw, Casey,' he said again. 'I almost daren't go in!'

'Don't be daft, mate!' Kieron urged. 'That thing's there for a reason, stupid. It's been put up there because you've done so well. Get on in there!' He gave him a nudge from behind to encourage him. 'And hurry up, will you? I'm freezing stood out here!'

The people inside must have heard us all deliberating, because just then one of the two double doors swung open to reveal a room that seemed full to bursting. It seemed everyone was there: John Fulshaw, of course; Justin's head of year at school, Richard Firth; his lovely teaching assistant, Helen King; the anger-management counsellor, Simon; plus Harrison Green with two other staff I recognised, who had worked with him from time to time; and then, finally, all of us – his 'family'.

He had been asked if he'd like to invite his mother to the ceremony, but he was adamant she wouldn't be welcome. 'She hasn't helped me though any of this,' he'd said, quite reasonably, 'so why should she share my party?' I'd been concerned, and still was, that he might regret that decision later but Mike too had been adamant about it. 'It's his day,' he reminded me. 'So it *must* be his choice. It's not up to us to try to pressure him in this. He has the right to decide who to invite.'

Seeing the sea of smiling and familiar faces seemed to dispel any lingering traces of shyness in Justin, and he went into the room, the three of us close behind him, and we all took our seats for the ceremony. A row of seats had been reserved for us, right at the front, and Justin quickly popped himself in between Mike and me so he wasn't the one right in the centre. Once again, as I sat down, I was moved by all the effort that had gone into celebrating this important day. To one side was a table that was laden with party food – the make-up of which was, as with the other details, something Justin had been asked to specify. He'd created his list and then emailed it to John, and, exactly as requested, the spread of his dreams was laid out in big mounds before us. There were pizza slices, sausages on sticks, jam sandwiches, crackers with peanut butter, cup cakes and – and I couldn't quite believe it when I saw them – even a plateful of crumpets and a toaster!

Above all this, there was even more evidence of celebration, in the form of clusters of balloons and coloured streamers. And Mike and I nudged each other at exactly the same moment, on both seeing the wall that was adjacent to the buffet, which had been completely covered with photographs of Justin, which I'd chosen and secretly emailed to John, earlier in the week. They were all such nice happy pictures, I'd thought, and looked even more so now they'd been blown up and displayed. It felt so good – such a lovely record of Justin's time with us – to see them all reproduced here.

The official graduation took place without delay, and Mike, Kieron and I listened very proudly as each member of the party took a turn to say a few words about Justin, and to rightly praise every little achievement. To an outsider who didn't know the child who'd first come to us, it might have seemed a bit too much – so much fuss about so little – but for *this* child it had been anything but. And I looked on with pride, not to mention the most enormous lump in my throat, as Justin stepped shyly forward to receive certificates and handshakes and accept the congratulations he really did deserve.

'Oh, my God, Mike,' I hissed, as the room finally erupted into a massive and sustained round of applause. 'I am going to lose it. I am, you know. I'm going to embarrass him now, for sure ...'

'You and me both, love,' he whispered back.

Justin's final prize was then presented, by John. It was a trophy – and a big one; no half measures here, it seemed – that was engraved with his name, underneath which was written, '*An outstanding achievement award for an outstanding young man*'.

'Now, then, young man,' John asked Justin, as he presented it, 'how about *you* saying a few words?'

I wanted to catch Justin's eye, then, so I could nod my encouragement. I felt certain that, like most boys of his age in this situation, making any sort of speech, however brief, would be a terrifying prospects. But to my surprise and pleasure, he looked John straight in the eye and nodded.

'Thank you everybody, for today,' he said, looking right around the room, and grinning as he held the trophy high above his head, to another inevitable round of cheers and whoops. 'I love this!' he added, and you could see that he really meant it. 'Thank you all *so* much. But I especially want to say thank you to Casey, Mike and Kieron. Oh, and Riley,' he turned to grin at me now, 'who can't be here. You've all done loads for me and put up with me and all my baggage – see, that's a good word, Casey! Got that from Simon! But anyway, thanks so much. I love you loads.'

At this, I was done for. I couldn't hold back the tears any longer. And I noticed Mike and Kieron were wiping their eyes too – the big softies – as I rushed up to give Justin a huge bear hug.

But Justin's celebrations weren't going to end with the presentation. We really wanted to celebrate at home too, as a family, so that we could really *get* home to him that he was properly, and permanently, a part of ours now, whatever the logistics of his next move.

We'd invited everyone we thought should be there with us. All Mike and my extended families who'd got to know

Justin since he came to us, plus our good friends and their children – all people who'd contributed positively to his life and who'd been such an amazing support to us, as well. John and the team travelled back to ours also, to continue the celebrations. In fact, the only person Justin didn't want to come back with us was Harrison – a notable exclusion, Justin explaining as his reason that Harrison being there would make it 'too official'. I didn't comment, but, in truth, I suspected that the real reason he didn't want Harrison there was because he, out of all of us, most represented the future. It would be him, after all, who would be accompanying Justin – and that big old suitcase of his – to his next home.

But we none of us wanted to dwell on such things; this was a day for the present, not the past *or* the future, and for today, at least, that was how it felt. The house was full of laughter and fun and games – just as it should be – and there was no further talk of what a watershed this was – no more points to be totted up, with chocolate and crumpets on a Friday, let alone what its passing *really* meant. And Justin seemed happy, *properly* happy, and it was really good to see. And at the end of it, Mike and I basked in a warm glow of satisfaction so that, for the moment, at least, life felt pretty good.

It was only when I popped upstairs a couple of evenings later, on my usual quest for dirty washing, that the reality of the new situation hit me hardest. Approaching Justin's room – he'd gone upstairs now to watch a movie – I was overtaken by Bob, who streaked inside ahead of me.

'Hey there, little fellow,' I heard Justin say softly. 'I'm gonna miss you when I have to go, aren't I?' There was a pause then, in which I could visualise him gently stroking Bob, before he spoke again, now in a voice that was even softer. 'Yes, I bloody well *am* gonna miss you, boy,' I heard him whisper. 'And you're gonna miss me, too, aren't you? Yes, you are. I *know* you are.'

Would he be able to articulate those feelings with us, I wondered? I so badly wanted that – for him to keep us all close. To feel secure in our love. Not to push us all away, as we'd repeatedly been warned to expect would happen. I tiptoed the rest of the way across the landing.

Chapter 22

It was a Friday morning, just a week after Justin's graduation ceremony, when the school rang.

'Mrs Watson?' I recognised the voice straight away. It was Richard Firth, Justin's head of year from school.

'Yes, it's me,' I said, already braced for the worst. You didn't tend to get calls from the high school in the middle of the school day just to update you how well your child had done in Physics, after all. Plus this was Justin. I wondered what had happened.

'We have concerns,' Richard said, 'so we thought we'd better get in touch. Sorry to land you with this now,' he continued. 'I know this is likely to be the last thing you want to deal with, what with the changeover of foster carers coming up. But there've been a couple of incidents that are causing concern, particularly during lessons when, I'm sorry to say, Justin's becoming rather disruptive again.'

'Oh, dear,' I said. What else was there *to* say, after all?
'What sort of things?'

'Just generally disruptive behaviours. He's been encouraging other pupils to misbehave; throw things and so on –
and doing a lot of very silly shouting out. It's also been
brought to my attention that he's not eating lunch.
Apparently he's been spending all his lunch money on
sweets and fizzy drinks, and we're concerned that it's all
part of a bigger overall picture of what seems to be atten-
tion-seeking behaviour.'

'I suspect you're right,' I said, recalling John's warning.
'What would you like me to do? Speak to him?'

'In the first instance, yes,' Richard confirmed. 'Perhaps
just let him know that he's still very much skating on thin
ice, especially where the school governors are concerned.
We really don't want to take things further if we don't have
to, particularly since he's been doing so well lately. So if we
could nip it in the bud, so to speak, with a few words from
you, then I'm sure we'd all feel a lot happier.'

'Oh, dear,' said Riley, who was round for coffee at the
time and had been able to hear my end of the conversation.
'It's like they said it would be, isn't it? That's so sad.'

I'd been filling Riley in about how John and Harrison
had warned us to expect a bit of a nosedive in Justin's
behaviour now his time with us was coming to an end; it
was, we'd been told, completely normal for this to happen;
it was a how a fostered child tended to protect their feelings
– they would try to make themselves unlovable so they
could more readily break their emotional ties. But the

reality was proving slightly more challenging than I'd imagined, not to mention the timing, which wasn't perfect. Riley was now at her due date – quite literally – and she could, and well might, go into labour at any moment. Which meant I needed, at least when David was at work, to be on hand. So the last thing I either wanted or needed right now was to be called away to help firefight a whole clutch of new behavioural problems.

Because the truth was that it wasn't just at school that there were concerns; things at home had become suddenly, inexplicably difficult, almost as soon as the graduation was over, and particularly after Justin's last meeting with Harrison Green, in which the new placement had been properly discussed. He'd been told all about the family, and had been shown pictures of them. A nice couple, by all accounts, childless, with two dogs. But it didn't really matter how nice they looked, did it? Going to them, however affable they were, meant leaving *us*.

But this was what we'd signed up for – this was what fostering was about: not slotting a child into convenient pockets of your life, but it *becoming* your life, more or less.

I sat back down with Riley and shook my head. 'It's panning out *exactly* how they told us it would,' I said. 'It's like he's got the textbook and we haven't. I had a headache the other afternoon, a real thumping one, you know? And when he came in from school and put the TV on at full blast, I went in and asked him to turn it down – as you do – and you know what he said?'

Riley shook her head and sipped her decaf. 'Go on, tell me.'

'He gave me a right look, and said, "Good! I hope you have a stroke!"' I picked up my own coffee and blew on it. 'Charming, eh?'

Riley frowned, and then seemed to consider for a moment. 'I know,' she said. 'He said something to me, too, actually. Me and David. On Monday. When he'd popped round while walking Bob. I wasn't going to bother to mention it, because, well, because it wasn't very nice, frankly, but –'

'Oh, don't worry about that,' I said. 'What did he say?'

'It was about you and Dad. Like you say, it's obviously part of the bigger picture, but I was just gobsmacked. We were talking about how when me and Kieron were little you got mad at us one time for putting dog leads on the rabbits and trying to take them for a walk down the street – remember that?' I nodded. I did. 'And then all of a sudden he comes out with, "Poor you. I feel sorry for you, being brought up my Mike and Casey." And I'm like "*What???*" and then he says "because they're crap parents" – something like that, anyway – and then "and I can't wait till I leave, because I hate them". Stuff like that. And I gave him what bloody for, as you can imagine! I was just *so* shocked to hear him say that, after everything, you know? I mean, yes, maybe six months ago, but *now*? I knew you wouldn't take it personally if I did tell you, but I was really, really cross with him. It was just so out of the blue – so unwarranted.'

'Except not,' I reassured her. She looked so embarrassed to even have passed it on, and I felt for her. 'It's exactly what John and Harrison told us would happen, isn't it? Which is all well and good, of course, and, no, of *course* I'm not going to take it personally, sweetheart. But what to do about it? That's my real concern.'

And it was a concern I voiced to Harrison Green once Riley had left. I would have shared it with John, but then I realised there was no point. Once Justin left us John would have no further involvement in his life. It was Harrison who would be taking over Justin's case once again, so I thought I had better pass on any potential future worries to him.

I also felt Mike and I needed some guidance. Did we rise to it? Discipline him? That certainly seemed to be the school's choice, and the one thing I really didn't want to end up happening was for him to get himself excluded again. Or did we just pretend it wasn't happening? Simply ignore it? What *was* the best way to tackle it? I had no idea.

'Respond to it, obviously,' was Harrison's advice. 'Tell him it's unacceptable, of course, but don't react emotionally. Don't give him any opportunity to escalate the conflict and get himself into more trouble with you or Mike. Just keep reassuring him you love him; that it's just the *behaviour* that's unacceptable. It's all just part of the process, so try to keep calm.'

Which pretty much dovetailed with my own instincts about it: that we needed to act as you would with a toddler.

Reinforce the good, keep a measured but consistent response to the bad. I wasn't sure Harrison would have been my first port of call on the advice front, but he had a lot more experience of both kids in care and of Justin, and in this I knew he was probably spot on. I hated to hear it – I didn't *want* Justin to sever his emotional ties with us – but everything Harrison said rang depressingly true.

'I can't bear the thought of that,' I confided to Mike when we were in bed that evening. 'I hate the whole idea of him thinking he must expunge us from his mind. I can see why he'd do that – why any child for whom everything is temporary would do that, but we can't let that happen with him. We just *can't*. If there's one thing that absolutely must come out of this is that he knows there are people here who love him unconditionally, and that we will always be here for him. *Always*.'

'He *will* know that,' Mike reassured me. 'If we just keep on doing what we're doing. He might not be able to show it right now – might have to act out the opposite, like he's doing. But deep down, he'll know it. And that's what matters. I know it's hard, love, but he's got to separate from us to some extent. He does have to leave us, after all.'

But there was one thing I didn't confess to Mike – not right then. That I felt terrible about all of it. Not just because things were rocky once again. But because, actually, I didn't want Justin to go. I wanted to keep him. It was as simple as that.

I suspected that Mike probably felt the same as I did about it all, but Mike being Mike – always far more practical and pragmatic than I was – whenever he saw me, as he'd put it, 'thinking too much', or looking sad, he would always respond by trying to 'gee me up', trying to get me excited about our next challenge, and its arrival, and would tell me how great I was doing. Which was great, and probably why we made such a good team, but, if I was honest, it did sometimes make me want to scream back at him, *'But I'm not doing well! I don't want a new challenge! I want to keep the one I've already got!'*

I called John Fulshaw the next day, and told him exactly how I felt, and then asked him if we could meet up in person. I needed to be clear about the options there were before talking it through properly with Mike. Happily, John had a meeting to attend not too far from us, only the next day, so we arranged that we could get together over coffee.

And as soon as I saw him, I realised I'd been right to voice my fears. He looked very much like he had things to tell me too.

'It wasn't something I was going to bring up,' he said, confirming it just as soon as we sat down. 'If I'm being scrupulously honest, it wasn't. Not least because I know this period's a tricky and emotional one for *any* foster parent, let alone one who's going through the process for the first time.'

'Bring up what?' I wanted to know. 'What haven't you told me? Don't tell me there's another grim secret lurking in the mix.'

I smiled as I said this, trying to keep the tone light. I didn't want him thinking I'd morphed into some sort of flake. But he shook his head.

'No more secrets. No, it's just something else that's happened. I had a call …'

'A call from who?'

'From Justin.'

'From *Justin*? Why would Justin call *you*? He doesn't even have your number, does he?'

Of course, as soon as I said this, I realised how stupid I was. Oh course he had access to John's number. Plus lots of others. It was pinned up on the fridge along with all my other regular numbers. 'And anyway,' I finished, feeling silly, 'he'd call Harrison, surely, if he had anything he wanted to discuss …'

'I think he did some research of his own,' John replied. 'Might have even got my number *from* Harrison, I suppose.'

I shook my head. 'No, he didn't.' I filled him in on my gaffe. Not that it mattered really. Why shouldn't he call John? No, he wasn't Justin's link worker. He was mine. But perhaps that was exactly *why* he wanted to speak to John. 'So what did he say?' I went on, intrigued now.

'In a nutshell? That he doesn't agree that he's actually "cured" yet. That he thinks he still needs your help to "sort himself out". He's basically asked if he can stay with you and do the programme again.'

Which put everything in the proper context, i.e. not the one we'd assumed. He wasn't playing up in order to create emotional distance from our family before leaving. He was playing up because he saw it as a way to be able to stay with us. 'Oh, my God …'

John sat back in his chair and shook his head. 'I know. And this is a first for me, Casey, I must say,' he admitted, echoing my own thoughts. 'And something that I imagine will be peculiar to this programme. I mean, it's not rocket science, is it? A kid in a stable placement is hardly likely to *want* to leave. And in the mainstream, then why on earth would they have to? They just wouldn't. A child would only leave a working placement to be returned to their own family, wouldn't they? So let's just say this is new territory for both of us.'

I was poleaxed to hear this. And also quite distressed. It was hard to find words to describe how it made me feel. 'Oh, John, that breaks my heart,' I said. 'To think that he actually *rang* you.'

'I know,' he said, nodding. 'I know.'

It was something that I wrestled with for days. I told Mike that night, about how I felt we needed to keep Justin. About how, far from wanting to break bonds with us to make the parting easier, he was actively trying to stop it happening at all. Which was, even if it took me a little time to realise it, perhaps the strongest indication that he'd made real progress during his time with us; he wasn't passively accepting things and wasn't displaying disturbed 'behaviours' either. He was trying to fix things; practising self-determination. It seemed to me he was trying to take charge of his destiny in a straightforward way, rather than self-harming or just passively accepting the inevitable. In short, he was no longer playing the victim.

But it was that, in the end, John's professional support notwithstanding, that most convinced me. We could drop out of the programme, and keep this one child right through till he was old enough to reach true independence, or we could do what we'd both trained to do, which was to support Justin through to his return to a mainstream foster placement, as had been the hope when he'd been placed at our 'last chance saloon'. And, in doing so, we could make way for another child or children, and then another, and perhaps another, potentially helping any number, as had been *my* hope and ambition when I'd originally left the unit at the school. Because, as Mike pointed out, the Watson clan weren't disappearing from Justin's life – weren't moving to Australia or anything, weren't abandoning him. And, just as with our own kids, *any* child who joined our family really did join it – if that was what they wanted, and I fervently hoped Justin did – for life.

And I also remembered, as I pushed my trolley round the supermarket that Saturday, looking for crumpets and that particular brand of hot chocolate Justin liked, that his new foster family didn't live that far away. Which meant that just as emotional bonds didn't break unless you cut them, so family traditions, such as ours, didn't need to either.

Chapter 23

'What shall it be then, Casey, do you think? Shall I wear the rugby shirt or my red hoodie? I can't make my mind up.'

It was a bright and frosty Saturday in the first week of November, and Mike was once again driving Justin to his mother's house for a contact visit. It was the first one since the terrible debacle back in August, and also, I realised, with a predictably heavy heart, probably the last one Mike or I would be involved in. I couldn't go with them this time, much as I wished that I could. By now, poor Riley was a week past her due date and I didn't dare stray too far from home in case she went into labour and needed me – as one of her birth partners – by her side.

It was a responsibility I took very seriously, as it was such a joy and a privilege to have been asked. I'd always sneakily hoped she might want me there, right from the start – what mother wouldn't? – but I wouldn't have dreamed of pushing myself forward, because that wouldn't have been right. It was a decision Riley and David would and should be making together, so all I could do was keep my fingers crossed they'd want me there too.

And happily, they did, and I couldn't have been more thrilled; to have the chance to witness my first grandchild coming into in the world – to say I had been over the moon is an understatement, really, and now the date was so close I could hardly contain myself.

But that of course meant I couldn't be there for Justin that day. And though I knew Mike could handle everything perfectly well without me, I still spent the time fretting about what was happening, and praying that this time it would all go okay. I didn't think I'd be able to keep a lid on letting my feelings be known if Janice did anything to hurt Justin today. I felt like a tigress with her cub, ready to attack anyone who upset him.

The visit had been a long time coming. Since the night-mare of the last visit, the no-contact order had remained firmly in place, and Janice had been subject to constant scrutiny. Social services had been working pretty much full time with the family, with support workers going in to visit on a weekly basis.

They'd kept me informed, too, letting me know that Janice had had things spelled out to her very clearly. She'd been told that unless she co-operated with social services fully, there was a real danger that she could lose her remaining children too, and quite possibly have her baby, now just born, put on the child-protection register. This had apparently shaken her up greatly, and it seemed that she had subsequently made a real effort to make some major changes in her life. This had included her cutting out most of her 'friends', admitting to the police that her middle son was possibly telling the truth about some form of abuse, though she still maintained that she couldn't remember the names of all the men who used to come around to take drugs.

She was now attending parenting classes and had undergone drug-rehabilitation treatment, so, all in all, it did seem as though she had turned a corner – one which I fervently hoped might be good news for Justin; perhaps it wasn't too late for their relationship after all.

I was certainly keen to share these positive snippets of news with him. Anytime I had an update about things going well I made a point of passing the good news on, and he did seem pleased to hear it, but there was always a slight reserve in his interest at such times, the understandable effect of all their previous encounters being that he simply couldn't afford to get his hopes up. Thinking about that now made my resolve even stronger. We occupied a privileged position in Justin's young life – he trusted us completely. So we must always remain constants – people with whom he *could* get his hopes up, secure in the knowledge that we would never, ever let him down.

But that glimmer of hope where his mother was concerned could never be completely extinguished, and with the evidence of her attempts to be a better parent (even if not, at this point, to him) it seemed to me that it mustn't be, either. Quite apart from anything else, Justin had his brothers, and it was so important that he maintain that connection.

So when, just a few days back, after a catch-up meeting with Harrison Green, Justin had suggested it might be time to phone his mum, I was quietly pleased that, once again, he'd taken charge of the situation, even though, at the same time, I was immediately anxious about the possibility of her rejecting him again. I obviously double-checked that this would be okay before allowing it, but as it turned out, the phone call went really well. Justin asked how she was and also asked about the baby, even laughing when Janice told him that she looked just like he had when he was born.

But after chatting for ten minutes, Justin suddenly passed the phone to me, putting me into something of a fluster.

'Go on, Casey,' he urged, pressing the phone into my hand. 'It's okay. She just wants to ask you if I can go see her.'

I felt uncomfortable and a bit flustered. I was really unsure how to talk to her. Which wasn't surprising, given the circumstances of our previous meeting. But I was surprised to hear her tell me that she wanted to thank me for everything we had done for Justin, and then came the bombshell: she completely floored me by also expressing her wish that Justin could stay with us for ever, because she knew how much he loved us.

I was floored. I didn't really know how to take this. I knew she meant well – everything in her tone made that obvious – but given all the progress since August, and with both of them, I couldn't understand why she'd say something like that. Surely her wish should have been that, eventually, he could be returned to *her*?

So I just told her that it had been a privilege to be able to care for him and what a lovely young man I knew he'd turn out to be, and agreed to her request that we drive him up to see her, while inside feeling so very sad.

And it seemed as though it was a bit of a week for it. Justin hadn't just offered an olive branch to his mother. He'd also, once the visit to his mum had been arranged, made peace with both of the men who might have fathered him, sitting down and writing letters to them both. This had come as something of a bolt out of the blue for me, as it had been something Justin had decided to do entirely unprompted. I had thought the blow of meeting the man at the snooker club had been a big one, but when Justin asked Harrison if he'd be able to pass some letters on for him, and told us the details, we were both so impressed by his maturity. He said he just wanted to let both men know that there were no bad feelings on his part and that should either of them want to get in touch with him in the future he would be very happy to hear from them. Seeing these – I'd sat with him and checked all his grammar and spelling before passing them on to Harrison – really brought a lump to my throat. And it was as much about his sense of acceptance as anything. He'd come to terms with the fact that perhaps he'd never know his real father, and was able to move forward without harbouring bitter thoughts.

It was clear evidence of just how far he had now travelled emotionally that he was able to be so rational and generous towards adults that had shown him nothing but neglect or misery.

'Do you know Justin, this is so grown up of you,' I'd told him as he carefully folded the letters and sealed the envelopes. 'When they get those letters, I bet they're going to feel very lucky to have you somewhere in their lives.'

He'd shrugged the shrug of a person resigned but not distressed. 'Well, it's up to them now, isn't it? The main thing's I feel like I've done something about it so I don't have to worry about it any more.' He shrugged again, and gave me a lopsided smile. 'Got it out, shook it out and put it away in my wardrobe, eh, Casey?' I nodded, choked and touched. 'And if they want me, they know how to find me now, don't they?'

I felt a real pang of compassion for him, and also a keen sense of injustice, at just how bloody unfair life could be. This boy could have had such a different outcome from day one, he really could, if just *one* of the adults in his life had been there for him. Properly there for him, selflessly and unconditionally – just as so many kids, my own included, could take for granted. But I pushed it to one side. He was dealing with it, wasn't he? And that was all he *could* do. Deal with it and move on.

I felt so proud of him. 'That's exactly right, love,' I said firmly. 'You've done your bit. So, no, you don't have to worry about it any more.'

But it turned out that I hadn't had to worry that morning, as I'd anxiously waved Mike and Justin off. When they returned a few hours later Justin was all smiles and laughter, so I could see straight away that the visit had gone well.

In the main, he was full of his little sister.

'Oh Casey, you should have seen her, she's so cute, she's gorgeous! An' she's not called Princess, she's called Gemma, and – hang on a minute.' He pulled off and began rummaging in his backpack. 'I've got a photo here somewhere that I can show you.' Finally he found it, and carefully extracted it, before holding it up proudly for me to look at.

'Oh sweetheart, she is just beautiful!' I agreed. 'She really is. And Gemma – what a lovely name! And you know, your mum was right. She really does look a lot like you did in your baby pictures.'

'I know' he gushed, 'and she's so strong, as well. She grabbed hold of my little finger and she wouldn't let go, she's got a right grip on her!'

We all laughed at this. 'And she's always smiling,' he went on. 'You saw her, didn't you, Mike?'

Mike nodded. I could see he was as caught up in Justin's mood as I was. 'I did mate,' he confirmed. 'Right little smiler, she is, isn't she? And with lovely blonde curls just like yours.'

I could see how much it meant to Justin, Mike saying that, and he sighed happily as he studied the picture. 'Aw,

Casey,' he said. 'You would have loved her, you would.' He then waggled the picture in front of me again. 'Do you have a frame I could use for this, by the way? I want to put it up beside my bed.'

I went into the kitchen to dig out a spare frame and Justin took his new favourite possession up to his room. 'Sounds like he's had fun,' I said to Mike, once Justin had gone.

'Oh, he did,' he agreed. 'And it was good for him, I think. I'm just pleased that his mum had the sense to lay off this time.'

'Me too,' I said, putting on the kettle to make him a coffee. Perhaps there was hope for them yet.

But it was hope of a different kind that Justin was harbouring, and, to my surprise it didn't centre on him. We were sitting in the living room, an hour or so later, the three of us, eating take-away pizza. This was a very rare treat in my house. I wouldn't normally ever let the kids eat in the living room – woe betide them – but as Kieron was at Lauren's, and Justin had no PlayStation buddy, and because this had been a pretty big day for him too, I relaxed my rule and we all shared our feast watching TV. Well, sort of.

'You know,' Justin remarked, out of nowhere, as we munched. 'I hope my mum manages to stay good now she's got a little girl.'

I put down the piece of Margherita I was holding, unsure of what he was getting at. 'How d'you mean, love?' I asked him, wiping the grease from my fingers.

'Well, I don't think she really liked boys. Not really. You know, because of all the bad men and stuff.' He seemed to consider a moment, staring into the middle distance. 'But she just seems so different now. I think she really loves this one, you know?'

I didn't really know what to say to this, but he expected a response. And I needed to supply one.

'Justin,' I said. 'I really think your mum loves *all* her kids. She just really struggled to cope when you were little. But she's stronger now and is doing so much better for herself. I think she'll stay good, my love, you'll see.'

Justin thought for a while before continuing. Then he nodded. 'I think you're right. I hope you are, too, because that's my little sister and no-one's gonna hurt her. Not even mum.'

Mike and I exchanged a glance as Justin bit into his pizza. 'I think she'll be fine, babes,' I told him.

He seemed to believe this. 'I do too,' he said firmly. 'It just makes me wonder though, Casey, why me? You know, why is it just *me* in care, and none of the others?'

This was the first time, to my knowledge, that Justin had ever asked this, and it was a question that everybody else, including me, had asked, but had never had any real answer to.

It hit me then that Justin was at last coming to terms with the fact that it was his mother who had left him in care. That nobody else was to blame for his situation; not him, not social services, just his mother. This must have been such painful knowledge for a child to have to digest.

But in doing so, he was taking a very important step towards some sort of peace.

'I really don't know, sweetheart,' I told him honestly. 'One day, when you're older, and you and your mum are able to talk grown-up to grown-up, she might be able to explain things a bit better to you. But what you *do* have to know is that it isn't your fault. It's never been your fault, not ever. And just remember – you have loads of people who love you, okay?'

Justin shoved a handful of chips into his mouth. 'What's not to love, eh?' he said, grinning.

But as well as having to accept the changes in the situation with his blood family, which he seemed to be doing admirably at the moment, Justin had also to prepare for a more immediate transition – that of gradually separating from the day-to-day life of our family, and becoming a part of a different one.

We had yet to meet the couple who were scheduled to become Justin's new foster carers. All we knew of them was that they were a middle-aged couple called Nick and Glynis Hanson, who had, after multiple miscarriages, given up trying to have children of their own. Instead, they had decided to foster. They'd only had one child placed with them, so far, but it had been for a very long time. John told me he had been with them for seven years in all, and was now grown up and living independently at university.

I had wondered straight away about how they'd cope with taking on Justin, remembering back to the real culture shock it had been for us – however willing – to go back to the round of dental appointments, heaps of dirty washing, piles of homework, messy bedrooms and the general full-on nature of having a child of that age back in your life.

But so far, it seemed, so good. He'd already met them once, with Harrison, on neutral territory, and had told me he'd found out they had two dogs, which excited him, but, more preoccupied, perhaps, with the looming visit to his mother's, he'd spoken little more about it. I hadn't pressed him, either. He would tell me about them, I knew, when he was ready, when the reality of going to live with them became a thought uppermost in his mind. In the meantime, the transition was being managed in a softly, softly manner, with frequent but short visits and little in the way of an agenda, the idea being that the change was completed gradually. The next step would be a sleepover, and then more protracted sleepovers, till eventually he'd be spending more time at theirs than at our house, and the process would finally be completed.

Today, the fourteenth past Riley's due date, which was killing me, Harrison had collected him from our house mid-morning, and he'd been over there for most of the day.

It was gone six when Harrison's car pulled up outside, and Justin came bundling in, smelling of cold fresh winter air and dog, and full of what a lovely time he'd had.

'That's brilliant news,' I told him, giving him one of my bear hugs. I found myself cuddling him more and more often, the closer I got to him going. I badly wanted him to know I was available for cuddling at all times. 'I'm so glad it went well,' I said. 'And how were the dogs?'

He grinned from ear to ear. 'They were lush, Casey!'

'That's fantastic news. And I'll bet they'll be really glad to have you to play with. Though poor old Bob's going to miss you terribly, you know.'

He frowned, but then considered. 'Maybe they could all meet each other – the dogs, like – then they could all become friends. I know! I could take them all for walks together, couldn't I?'

'I dare say you could,' I agreed, herding him into the kitchen. 'Anyway, what kind of dogs are they?'

'I'm not sure,' he said. 'Bit big. Much bigger than Bob. Alsations maybe, I think. One's called Rufus and the other one's called Blue, and they're both, like, *mad*. And Nick said that next time I go – when I stay overnight – we can take them to the beach for the day. They love playing in the sea, he said, and getting really wet. But he said you have to be careful when they come out, or they get you. Like, *completely* soak you, when they shake off all the water.'

'Rather you than me, then!' I said, laughing as I pulled out a plate and mug for him. 'I think I'd prefer to –' But then I stopped speaking, because Mike was in the kitchen doorway, grinning strangely.

'That was David,' he said, gesturing to the phone in his hand. 'Our Riley's just gone into labour.'

Chapter 24

Deep breath, I said to myself slowly. Deep breath. It had finally happened. The big day had come. I'd been in a mad panic, more or less, since Riley's due date had come and gone, but, actually, now that it was finally here, I began to feel a calmness descend.

Which was just as well. I had been booked in as her birthing partner – along with David, obviously – so I had things to do. From now on it was action stations.

'Right,' I said to Mike, grinning broadly at Justin as I did so. 'Shout up to Kieron, will you, love? And get him downstairs. Then I'll need the list from the drawer in my bedside table.'

But Mike wasn't really listening. He was preoccupied himself, and showing every sign of turning into the proverbial headless chicken, picking up his car keys, putting them down again, grabbing his coat and generally getting in a flap. Not like Mike at all, but then, he'd never been a grandparent-to-be before, either, and I could see he was going to need direction.

'Mike!' I said again, only more firmly this time. 'We've got plenty of time, and everything is already organized. Now, can you *please* go and fetch Kieron?'

I turned to Justin again who was by this time looking less 'Oh, how exciting! Riley's going to have a baby!' and more 'Help! This house seems to be in meltdown!' I placed a reassuring hand on his shoulder and squeezed it. Didn't matter how far he'd come, Justin still needed routine. And so he needed to be reassured there still was one in place. 'It's alright, sweetheart,' I said to him soothingly. 'Everything's arranged for you. It's just like we spoke about a couple of weeks back, remember? Mike and I are going to go to the hospital to be with Riley, and Kieron and Lauren are going to stay here and look after you.'

He nodded, but still looked anxious. 'Okay,' he said. 'But will you be home again tonight?'

'I don't know, love,' I told him truthfully. 'Babies can sometimes take their time coming. But you'll be *fine*. Lauren will be sleeping over too, don't forget. And she and Kieron will make your tea and breakfast and everything. And I'll call you, I promise. Right before your bedtime. So I can keep you up to date how everything is going.'

He nodded again, and I could see he was looking a bit less fretful. He'd be fine, I knew, with Kieron and Lauren. I'd already written down everything they needed to know, after all. What food to make, what all the timings were and so on. Though, happily, it was going to be Sunday

tomorrow so all the instructions about school I could now
cross off the list.

'Mum!' Kieron said, now rattling down the stairs behind
Mike. 'Make sure you call me. Every hour, okay? I don't
care how late it gets, just make sure you do. I won't be able
to sleep unless I know Riley's okay.'

I reassured him I would, feeling a great surge of maternal love. It was so moving to see how much my children
cared about each other. And then another thought struck
me, about my first foster-son, too. He was about to be a
part of one of the biggest events of our lives. If anything
would bind him to us, that would. I kissed both him and
Kieron and promised them both that we'd call, and then
the two of us shot out of the door.

We arrived at the maternity hospital just as Riley was being
linked up to a monitor. She'd actually been well into her
labour when she'd arrived there and was already having
contractions every minute.

But it was a first baby and I knew that contractions every
minute didn't necessarily mean the baby was coming any
time soon. So while poor Mike paced the waiting room for
a long lonely three hours, I did my best birth-partner-mum
bit, alongside an anxious David, mopping Riley's brow,
passing her the gas and air mouthpiece and telling her how
brilliantly she was doing.

Anyone who has ever witnessed a birth would I'm sure
agree with me when I say that, watching the birth of my
first grandson, at 11.15 p.m. on that late November

Saturday, was thrilling and moving beyond words. I couldn't remember the last time I had cried so much. I was so proud of Riley that I couldn't contain it, and to hold that little scrap of new life in my arms made me cry even more. It's a wonder I didn't completely soak him.

Mike was in with us moments later, the business end having been sorted and, of course, he and David started crying as well. In fact I don't think I'd ever seen Mike cry quite that hard. Within seconds he was sobbing his heart out.

It took a full five minutes for him to regain some composure, and when he did, presumably feeling a bit abashed by his tearful display, he leaned close to Riley's left ear and he spoke. 'You know, love,' he said, 'he is gorgeous. He really is. But don't you think his ears are a bit like Uncle Glynn's?'

Riley, being Riley, was not having that. She gave him a spirited left hook and then delivered her verbal counter-blow. 'Yeah, right, Dad,' she said, grinning. 'And I can cope with it, just as long as he isn't landed with your nose!'

Which had me filling up again, of course, and reaching for the tissues. I slipped out then, and, as promised, I phoned home.

They say everything happens for a reason, and perhaps the birth of baby Levi had been a great feat of timing, because, as with any family upheaval, such as the birth of a new baby, the first couple of weeks went by in a kind of blur. With Riley and I being so close, we spent a lot of time together and, while on the surface I was bustling about, helping her to manage, inside I knew my daughter was actually managing magnificently on her own; she seemed such a natural at this whole motherhood lark. It would be a couple of years before I fully realized how much of a natural, but in the meantime I was happy enough to take a zillion photos and bask in a warm flush of grandmotherly pride.

And most importantly, from the point of view of Justin's own upheaval, it perhaps meant I was a little less intensely anxious as well, having another little boy to distract me. Which could only be a good thing, from all our points of view, as it made the transition just that little bit less stressful.

As did finally meeting his new family. Levi was two weeks old when we I finally got to meet the Hansons, who turned out to be absolutely lovely. By now we were dropping Justin round to them ourselves – it seemed crazy for Harrison Green to have to keep doing it, and, besides, it was our hope, even if the Hansons didn't yet know it, that Justin would find it easy to pop round and visit once he had transferred to live with them full time.

This made sense, of course, from the point of view of his emotional stability, and though we'd never thought to ask it did occur to both of us that the location of the placement, which was close to us geographically, might have been a factor in the decision-making process. And not only for reasons of him being able to keep in touch with us. It also meant he wouldn't have to move to yet another school – a harrowing enough experience for any child of his age, let alone one with his array of problems.

It was important, therefore, that the four of us got along, and they'd invited us to pop in and join them for coffee that afternoon, when we dropped Justin off for a sleepover.

'Isn't it awful,' I told Mike, over a take-away curry later on that evening. It felt weird. With Justin at the Hansons overnight, and Kieron having gone off out somewhere with Lauren, it was our first night alone and commitment-free in what felt like ages. Just the two of us and a blow-out meal in front of the TV. 'And I feel ashamed to admit it,' I admitted, 'so don't tell. But I think I was secretly looking for reasons not to like them.' I spread my palms. 'Isn't that mad?'

Mike grinned. 'I wouldn't have expected you to be any different,' he said.

'Hey!'

'I mean, is there any hope they'll ever be good enough for him, after us? After *you*?'

'Mike, that's a terrible thing to say! Don't take the mick!'

'Only kidding,' he said. 'But you forget – I know how your mind works, love. And I'm not being sarcastic. I know this is hard. When you put so much into something – or some*one*, in this case – of course you want it to be special. You want him to feel you're special. That he's going to miss you. Not have him stroll off with the Hansons without so much as a backward glance.'

'That's the truth of it, I guess,' I admitted. 'You're spot on. But they seemed lovely, didn't they? I think he'll be happy there, don't you? And you know why? Because they really seemed genuinely fond of him, too. Not just professionally caring – not just being carers by numbers – I got a real sense that they were so down to earth and loving. Like they really wanted to make a difference to his life.'

Mike slipped his arm around me and pulled me in for a hug, perhaps sensing that beneath my positive exterior there was still a part of me that just wasn't quite ready to let him go.

'You'll still be a hard act to follow, love,' he whispered, bless him.

It had been strange, having Levi come into our lives just as Justin was preparing to leave it, and I wasn't sure, in the first days, with all the comings and goings, if all the attention now focussed on the baby would make the parting easier or harder for Justin. On the one hand there was the whole new topic of conversation, my repeated comings and goings back and forth to Riley and David's place and the way the family routine had so changed, and on the other there was the to-ing and fro-ing Justin was doing too, as 'home' became something of a moveable feast – as his visits to his new home increased in frequency and his time at his current home lessened.

Levi must have been not much more than three or four weeks' old, though, when I realized the concept of home, in this instance, really didn't have to mean bricks and mortar. Yes, it was obviously crucial that Justin settle well in with his new family, but I still fretted constantly that in our encouragement to that end, he didn't feel he was being pushed out of ours.

But I needn't have worried. He'd come home from school for tea one day – though he'd be going home to the Hansons straight after – when Riley arrived at the house with Levi.

She was looking tired, but also happy, and was still coping well, taking everything that came her way in her stride.

'Hey, Justin!' she said, when she arrived to find him home. 'How nice to see you – and perfect timing, too! D'you want to give Levi his bottle for me, so I can put my feet up for ten minutes and have a bit of a natter with Mum?'

Justin blinked at her, obviously still digesting what she'd said, and seeing the attendant expression on his face was priceless. It was also a reminder of how far we'd come, for it was a look, if slightly nervous, of stunned delight.

'Come on,' Riley coaxed. 'Come and sit yourself down on this chair' – she pulled one out from under the kitchen table for him – 'and get yourself comfy while I heat up his bottle.'

Justin did as instructed and, while Riley warmed the bottle, I took Levi from his pram and placed him very carefully in Justin's arms. Happily, Levi seemed just as happy to be in Justin's as anyone's and, once the bottle was warm and Riley had shown Justin how to angle it, he sucked away happily, a dreamy, far-away look on his face.

But it was Justin's face – though neither Riley nor I would ever have considered mentioning it – that mesmerised the two of us the most. He was sitting there, as gentle as any loving brother could be, and feeding Levi with tears in his eyes.

I shed a lot of tears myself over those next couple of weeks.

I'd always known that fostering would be a bit of an emotional rollercoaster, and that upheavals such as this one were all a part of the package, but I was still shocked, as was Mike, by how much like a bereavement it felt to be losing him.

But, little by little, it was happening – he was distancing himself, and though I knew intellectually that this was what he had to do, to cope, I still felt the rejection very keenly.

John Fulshaw tried hard to counsel me about it, and to reassure me, but I still couldn't help reliving all the stages we'd been through and wondering what we – what I – could have done differently. I suppose what I really wanted was the thing I couldn't have: I wanted him to show me just how much he missed me – would continue to miss me – which was precisely the thing he couldn't allow himself to do.

He was also, and John felt he had to keep stressing this to me, a profoundly damaged child who'd suffered a great deal of rejection and who, John explained, would now be unable to form anything but superficial relationships with another human being.

'But I'm different!' I wanted to yell at him, though I didn't. Was I really? Probably not, but that didn't help me keeping a kernel of hope alive that for Justin I might be – we all might be. If not right now, then maybe one day.

'You have to harden yourself up somewhat,' he stressed, and kept on stressing, over a coffee in my kitchen, in mid-December. 'Because all placement endings are going to feel a bit like this, Casey. That's the nature of the work. That's how it's always going to be.'

I looked out of the kitchen window and the coral-tinted sky, which, to my mind, looked heavy with snow. Or at least seemed to. None was forecast, so perhaps it was just me. I did a lot of wishful thinking about snow at this time of year. It was almost Christmas and, once again, I was going overboard. Perhaps, I thought, looking at the front-garden fairy lights twinkling (even though it wasn't even quite dark yet, I'd put them on), I was going even more overboard than usual. Not only because we had a baby's first Christmas to get excited about, but also to fill the big hole Justin had left.

And I knew I must make the effort to recharge my batteries, because as John left he told me it was an order. 'You and Mike will have two weeks to relax,' he explained. 'And then you'll be offered your next child.'

I waved him off, feeling the biting December cold swirl around my legs, and watched as he unlocked and climbed into his car.

Just before he left, he rolled down the driver's window. 'Expect fireworks in January,' he said …

Epilogue

So just how has Justin progressed since leaving my family? Well, his new placement lasted two years before, sadly, breaking down. As John had warned, it turned out he felt unable to bond with them, and after a couple of years he started talking all the time about being moved back into a children's home. He eventually left the Hansons and transferred to one, where he remains, detached but settled, to this day. He's currently working as a gardener.

Though it's probably true that Justin will never fully engage with society as an adult, he is still very much a part of our family, and comes to see Mike and I every week. As for Riley, she and David have three children now, Levi, Jackson and Marley Mae. Justin still spends every Christmas Day with the whole family, at Riley and David's house, and loves the kids as much as they adore him, always calling him their 'Uncle Justin'.

Kieron and Lauren are still together, which has made us all so happy, and are expecting their first baby this year. Justin's excited about that too and only recently confessed that he keeps a scan photo of the baby in his wallet.

As for Justin, well, he's seventeen now and, I'm happy to report, still maintains contact with his birth family. He sees his mother and brothers twice yearly and has seemed to have sort of accepted the fact that they'll never be a 'proper' family, really. He still gets yearnings for his mum sometimes but what he tends to do is to call me and we talk them through together. As for Gemma, well, that's a rather lovely footnote to it all – now she's old enough, they talk all the time on the phone.

In general, for all of *us*, it's quite simple. To Justin, we're just Mike and Casey and we will always be there for him, as will Riley and David, Kieron and Lauren – the whole clan. But if you want to sum things up, perhaps the best way is to say that he refers to Kieron and Riley as his step-brother and step-sister. Which, for me and Mike at least, says it all.